Anthem for a Burnished Land:

WHAT WE LEAVE IN THIS DESERT
OF WORK AND WORDS

A DESERT MEMOIR

SHAUN T. GRIFFIN

JUNIPER

First published in 2016
Juniper is an imprint of Southern Utah University Press
Cedar City, Utah

© Shaun T. Griffin 2016

ISBN Paperback: 978-0-935615-50-0
ISBN Hardcover: 978-0-935615-51-7
Library of Congress Control Number: 2015960161

Layout and design by Bridgette Burr
Cover photography by Shaun T. Griffin, design by Bridgette Burr

Printed in the United States by Lightning Source

Acknowledgments

I would like to thank the following people whose goodwill and encouragement kept me at the desk: Margaret Dalrymple for suggesting this memoir; Ben and Karen Wesner who found us that first snowy porch; the late Jess Hayashi—first and best friend, wherever you are—and the Hayashi-Solomon family for waiting so long; the Community Chest crew—Erik, Paula, Shannon, and Cindy who were almost there from the beginning; poets Gary Short, Gailmarie Pahmeier, Tom Meschery, William Wilborn, Steven Nightingale, Bill Cowee, and Stephen Liu, and the essayist Robert Leonard Reid, without whom this poet would be greatly diminished; Douglas Unger, brother in the art; Robert Laxalt and Monique Laxalt for insisting I could; Cameron Sutherland for her careful proofreading and suggestions; Katja Lektorich who made it whole; Wendell Berry for caring, always; Robert Blesse, formerly of Black Rock Press, who has preserved most Great Basin poetry; stalwart friends Paul and Maxine Cirac, Ann Holloway, and until most recently, her late husband, Jack, who brightened every summer; Squeek LaVake; and Lucy Bouldin, librarian in a labyrinth of extremes.

It goes without saying that the writers who reach deepest are the ones rarely seen: Ismael Santillanes, Cornell Wilkins, Billy Weyer, Chip Evans, Bobby Gonzales, J. Cole Johnson, Michael Smith, Glynn Scott, and the dozens of men who journeyed into the maw of poetry. And to Chaplain Al Fry, for being there.

This story was written in many places—Puerto Viejo and San Jose, Costa Rica; Johnson, Vermont; Santa Fe, New Mexico; Mendocino and Mission Viejo, California—and sometimes it was written when I was flying or traveling across this wide-open Nevada. Even though it was recalled from far away, the stones never receded. The place of home remained and it drew me back much as I am drawn to its telling.

Thank you to everyone at the Vermont Studio Center where some of this story was written.

To Richard Shelton, your magnanimous example let so many of us follow you onto the yard.

To my friend and photographer Nolan Preece, who made the images in this book possible, *un fuerte abrazo.*

To Joe-Anne, Rose Marie, Baron, and Howard, my deepest thanks for your "lovingkindness" across the miles.

To Hayden, who taught us how.

And finally, to Harriet "Hank" Cummings, for her fierce determination to adjudicate right from wrong.

My greatest debt is to the many poets and storytellers beyond this time who have shaped my journey with their words.

Grateful acknowledgment to the following editors where these essays and poems first appeared: "Waiting in the Dental Line," *Red Rock Review* (2014); "Dressing for Fire," forthcoming in *Weber—The Contemporary West*; "Anthem for a Burnished Land," in *Nevada Review*, (spring 2011).

Contents

I

September Light   9
Waist-Deep in Pyramid Lake   19
Braiding the Wind   23
The Trail to Hobart Reservoir   33
Building Community in the High Desert   43
Learning from the Artists   53
Down the Hidden Path to Poetry: Surrender on the Yard   61
Making Do   71
Mountains Above Manzanar   79
The Board of Pardons Hearing   85
Trying to Answer His Question   93

I I

A Mountain Schoolhouse   111
The Soprano Behind the Plate   121
The Woman and Her Children   131
When Jake Came Wheezing to the Door   139
The Bloody Money   149
American Flats   157
Renegades   165
When the Ones You Love Go Down   175
Forty Words for Brown   179

I I I

Passing Through Nevada   193
Pushing to Meet the Need   197
Stepping Outside the Prison   203
The Echo Skittering Through Town   209
Looking Through the Tourists   215
Dressing for Fire   223
Losing the Library   231
Waiting in the Dental Line   237
The Tarantula Crossing at Devil's Gate   245
Through the Saffron Light   249
Anthem for a Burnished Land   255

for Debby, Nevada, and Cody—
whose hands kept me close
in the dust and wind

For those outside
            its sphere—
the desert
            has a rosary:
            come,
live in this place,
see how long
            it takes.

STG

The land gave up its meaning slowly
as the sun finds day by day
a deeper place in the mountains.

John Haines

I

September Light

There may be no better light on the Comstock than when the leaves begin their migration and the quail have nursed their young from the nest. It is then I think of my predecessors, the hundreds and hundreds who came to this mountain in search of something more. Unlike them, I came in search of quiet, and this afternoon with the cricket, the fly, and the leaf, it is the place of my desire.

In August the light descends further and further south and hangs on a low arc for most of the day. By now—mid-September, it has changed everything: the rabbit brush is saffron, the locust seeps to yellow, and the Virginia Range has a burnt tint. You cannot live here without the specter of light: it draws you closer and closer to an orbit of daily rituals that must be performed to stay alive. Of course, the light is a signal: weather will change soon. You must prepare.

In this stillness there is anticipation: the hauling, splitting, and stacking of wood. Just today, my nearest neighbors were wedging rounds of pine and almond into their backyard hutches. I have let oak rounds season for years—they are still too hard to crack open with a maul. This will go on for some time. Weather will threaten and there will be more cautious planning: load the porch with kindling and dry rounds and then some rest before the necessity of heat.

*   *   *

Of all the places we *could* have moved to in northwestern Nevada, we chose Virginia City out of caprice: one of my students at Western Nevada College, Karen Wesner, suggested we look at a house her friend had built. It had been sitting vacant for a year. It was the middle of winter, January 1980, and two feet of snow covered the deck of the small house. Debby opened the door and we said, "We'll take it," then we ferried furniture for three weeks in the rain and snow.

I knew nothing of this climate and certainly not its light. In this, too, I must have been like my predecessors: migrants to a mountain with little understanding of its requirements.

As histories go in the American West, Virginia City has a long one, most of it admirably chronicled by the many journalists who called it home: Alf Doten, Dan DeQuille, Sam Clemens (then), and later, Lucius Beebe and more. Their stories read like cartographies from a frontier planet—they were fresh, exciting, and exaggerated at every opportunity. *Roughing It* is surely the funniest of those accounts. Twain left, of course, but not before fomenting the idea of the Comstock, and a hundred and fifty years later, this little town is still the nexus of gold and its gatherers.

I inhaled in awe at this cultural history: 15,000 people at its height in the 1860s, 64 pubs, four schools, an opera house and yes, a Chinese dump over which our house was built. When the snow from that first winter melted I tried to dig holes for a fence. The further I dug, the more oyster shells I tossed along with the occasional opium bottle, ceramic beer bottles, and countless prescription vials in all colors and sizes. But the earth would not relent—it was dry and hardened. Nothing I did seemed to loosen the rocks from their grip. It was then, with blisters and a sore back, that I began to understand something of this physical place: if you cannot tolerate the extremes of weather and what they portend, you should leave after one harsh season.

*   *   *

This time of light is a gift, a respite from those extremes of heat and cold. It is a false hopefulness, a short reprieve of nearly perfect weather. This September has been particularly beautiful with almost no wind to whip the dust from the sills. In the arid West, light is refracted through very few water molecules, which makes it intense, and the sky the blue of a robin's egg. At 6,200 feet this sky opens to a view of 130 miles or more and gives the light a place to roam. Multiple ranges disappear into deeper and deeper pools of brown and purple until finally the desert between those mountains washes into the horizon.

This is open country; there is little to hide behind. Nor is convenience close. Twain had more exotic food on this mountain than we do—an irony he might still be laughing at. The oyster shells below the house were shipped here from San Francisco by train and stage. Beyond them, rusted cans, bedsprings, broken glass, coins, shoe leather, the detritus of a town in its heyday. All these remnants of self-reliance—what did it take to live here?

*   *   *

First I had to get a car that would intimate traction. Driving through South Lake Tahoe, I saw a Land Cruiser muddied from headlight to tailpipe. The driver had just come over the Rubicon, an off-road trail from the Sierra Foothills to the west shore of Lake Tahoe. I asked if it was for sale. Two weeks later my girlfriend, Debby, and I were lying under the car trying to install taillights. We put the hard top back on and the owner taught me how to lock the hubs and switch into four-low. We drove it home from Eureka, California, and it almost ran as good as it was purported to do.

Cars had always been a part of my life—in the driveway was a '49 Chevy woody that my father and I restored. Its grill had so much chrome you couldn't look at it in the sunlight.

That Land Cruiser was nearly indestructible—well, except for the brakes, which worked most of the time. Snow was not a problem, and soon I packed the essentials, sleeping bag, Hi-Low jack, tow chain, cables, and tools. It was not a comfort machine. Driving across Highway 50 in winter, snow coming in the doors, Debby kept the sleeping bag over her knees with the floor heater on high, which is why we had our down jackets on. Gas was cheap and six cylinders were all you needed to get anywhere in the West.

*　　　　　*　　　　　*

I didn't know there was an identity associated with being in the "West" when I moved here. I assumed it was a place like any other: except that you made your living in the shadow of big mountains—45 peaks over 10,000 feet in Nevada, and Mt. Davidson at 7,800 feet out my back window. The USGS has a survey marker on the peak and several intrepid miners have scribed their names on metal poles stuck into the rock. When I scale that mountain and look east it is like the first time every time. I imagine those names, the history below me and the vast emptiness beyond with trepidation: surely their record has forged mine, and then I'm shook back to the dust and wind. Once I climbed that peak in such hail my Dalmatian whined at the small stones pelting him. We hid under the one tree until the storm broke and then I started into wind at a 30-degree angle but could not fall down.

I did not need a field guide to be struck by the obvious beauty of this place. Without being able to say it, that too was what drew me. It is easy to be attracted to the mountains and lakes of the Sierra Nevada. I had hiked them since I was a boy, in fact nearly lost my life in the 1968 snowstorm in Mineral King. But I was completely unprepared for the high desert and I would not have said it is there I choose to live—at least when I first arrived in Nevada. My only thought was escape: I drove that Land Cruiser to ski every weekend I could—the great empty landscape was too foreboding to ride out alone and surely required some other alphabet to speak its silence. I was a city kid—what did I know about landscape? That was a breath I took in college, a field trip but not a place in which I would live.

My first winter in Nevada was spent in Yerington, a farm valley southeast of Virginia City. After teaching in the satellite campus of Western Nevada College, I ran the onion fields to the tailings from the Anaconda mine. Many of the people I taught had worked there for years. One man had spent his life in the mine and now it was closed. His wife was a Shakespeare scholar at the high school. What did it mean to be a *former* employee of that company after 28 years? He was too young to retire and too far from a city where he might find work. This wasn't what he expected. There were no plans for this. Each day he came to me and asked, "What can I do? Nobody *needs* a former mine shift manager." I must have looked the fool to him: half his age, hardly an adult, and couldn't see beyond the leach pond to make any sense of this, his life.

He took classes, tried to find another occupation, something he could do with his newly found freedom. In the end, it was the waiting, the boredom, and the not knowing that was hardest. He was a man of quiet courage: in the nine months we spent together he never asked for pity, never wanted anything more than a chance.

In one of those ironies that belie the sorrow of circumstance, his wife taught the man who published my first book of poetry. How could this be, such torment in a family, and yet she reached many young minds: another of her students received his Ph.D. in English at Stanford. She was a legend in the valley and equally strong in spirit. She never doubted her husband would find his way back, never hinted that I would fail him. This was trust—the man she married trying to find a future with a newcomer. Somewhere in his eyes I began to learn about the endurance it took to stay alive in this physical place.

This was part of coming to the desert: learning to be vulnerable where there were little more than cottonwoods. At least his version of the story was like that and because it was his version, it became part of mine. First you must pay attention: if the script for your life begins to erode, write something in the dust. I left that valley to work in the capital city of Carson—out of boredom and maybe fear that I would never leave. What I wanted to do was write and be nearer those I loved. Not so much different than he.

If it was September when we met, I did not see this light on the open-pit mine of Yerington. I did not recognize its sumptuous quality. When winter came to the valley, it was brown and the crops were gone. Ice filled the irrigation canals. But I saw horses: a friend was learning to fly and she flew me over range after range and we buzzed the horses. The valley was different then: it was like sitting on Mt. Davidson, high above Virginia City. The view was infinite and all of the land below looked like a rolling brown canvas, the ridges gnarled like a topographic map. At the higher elevations, the peaks turned to green or something like green: piñon and juniper above the sage. Not quite the Sierra, but a change in the color below. And water, scarce as it is in Nevada, snaked its way to Lake Lahontan, the reservoir built for the Fallon farmers. Being a prankster she lifted her hands off the joystick and said, "It's yours."

"What's mine?"

"The plane, stupid."

No wonder the horses were running.

* * *

Water and light, these two would haunt me when we touched down. My friend gave me an aerial freedom, something I had never known. In the sky over this dry land, the earth began to look like brown water—it moved below us in huge rivulets. When darkness started we buzzed the small strip outside of town to wake the sheriff and turn on the runway lights. No sign of him. She peered below: was it this street, the one with the building to the right? Did she dare bring the plane down in the fading light? Never excited, she dropped in just above the runway, turned and set the plane down. She could have landed it with a flashlight below. This, too, made the emptiness seem comforting—it took belief in one's skill to navigate it. I remembered one of my teachers in grad school: "You should learn to fly, Shaun. It's much safer than racing cars."

* * *

I was living in a rented house on the outskirts of Yerington. There were cottonwood rounds out back. I borrowed a wedge and maul and began the annual search for warmth. Most people mocked cottonwoods—quick, hot heat—but soon they were ash and the heat was gone. It didn't matter to me. I sat at the hearth and stared into the blue flame—probably in a trance—so lovely was the picture of this elemental process. A fire cut from earth, split with hands and rising over steel and brick.

I had a card table in the kitchen. By night I wrote short stories, and even though there was almost nothing in the house to eat, I was as happy as a pumpkin in a patch. My life had cadence: I worked, wrote, and skied. There was nothing in the dust but time.

I had a flea market amplifier that found two stations out of Reno. When the rock and roll went off the air I called my friend Jess, who left for northern California. "How are you," I asked in the darkness? Silence, protracted silence, and then the slow admonition:

"I'm hanging on." He killed squirrels most of that winter to supplement his diet and burned manzanita—very hot and almost nothing to it—but poor is poor and he was trying to run a school for wayward adolescents. We thought about our choices—how you leave a place, how you make a new place home, how in the alchemy of youth you settle for what you have.

One night after a long soak in the hot springs, my friends and I draped our towels over the real furnace, only to wake to the stifling smolder of rayon and cotton. The house and its residents nearly returned to the ground. After the wind blew most of the smoke out, I left for vacation, thinking all would be fine with the house. In my ignorance, I turned off the heat. By the time I got home the house was flooded. For a week the carpets hung on the fence, frozen like giant brown squid. The neighbors got the greatest laugh watching me sleep in the car. It took days to find a plumber who would drive that far to crawl over the ice beneath the house. By the time the landlord arrived, I was politely asked to leave.

My neighbor was a game warden. He came home once a week with long stories about hunters and their prey. Again, I didn't have a reference point—what was he *doing* in that wide expanse of land? Why were there people trying to poach large game? Why must he carry a rifle in his cab? The answers were many: he had been shot at, threatened, chased and yet found some peace in being able to roam the high desert. He felt an obligation to protect the wildlife and those who safely hunted. He had a nobility of purpose like the shift manager in the mine. Each was doing work that required skill and intention that time alone would not replace. This parallel universe of labor stood in contrast to the labor I knew in the city. This was old labor, hunting, mining, things many people had given up in the rush of progress. Something else for the newcomer to distill.

After I got kicked out of the flood, my roommate and I found a trailer with direct-drive plumbing and one east-facing window. The sun rose over a Formica counter and we learned the rituals of being bachelors in a small town—don't date, don't look up, and get out for your fun. He was in love with a good Catholic girl from Vegas and I with a Belgian from LA. We read and talked and burned the hours with reminiscences of our homes in other states. He worked for the

Soil Conservation Service and driving the fields, came upon a red-tail with a jackrabbit in its claws. That night we fed four baby rabbits with eyedroppers. The old timers said they would never last but they did and he freed them in the trenches of wild anise and asparagus.

Coming home through Wilson Canyon a shadow drifted over the Land Cruiser then bent its wings to snick the back of another jack-rabbit in full terror: a golden eagle with the fluff of its prize. Predator and prey. The twin tracks of discovery and loss: this was a way of life.

My roommate grew up on the South Texas border. His mother was the first Mexican Head Start director in Texas. All of her children had gone to college—she knew what hunted those who came across the Rio Grande. Years later, when his second child was born with a blue rose of veins across her forehead, he took it in stride. The specialist clipped the tangle of vessels from her brow to leave her sight in the other eye. In this, he was like my pilot friend—unflappable and perfectly suited to the land.

I didn't want to leave him when I left for the capital, but jobs were few and we parted—he farther east to Battle Mountain and I to Washoe Valley.

*   *   *

Sometimes I joke with Debby: you should have never come to Nevada. You get lizard skin four weeks after you arrive and then the nosebleeds start. When she arrived in the fall of 1979, we rented a house in Washoe Valley. She was uneasy with the stillness of her new home: her counseling job at the alternative high school in Reno left her with more free time than she had had in years. In Fullerton, during her last year of grad school, she worked three jobs, commuted halfway across the LA basin to facilitate school desegregation, teach counseling, and run a preschool. She had prepared for a very different life from the one she found herself in. She came here out of a devotion that was not fully known to either of us. We wanted to be together, near the mountains, and not in the busy center of traffic and smog that was our recent home.

She busied herself with building our bed from piñon pine. It was about three feet off the ground and filled some of the cavernous bedroom. At Christmas she asked our friends to bring an ornament for the tree, the tree I could barely drag through the front door. We still have some of them. I started to hear about a woman who taught in one of the satellite centers at the school. Before long, she brought Lisa Hixson to the house—blond, curly hair, and radiant. She, too, had just come from Southern California. One by one I met Debby's colleagues at the school—all of them drawn to the possibility of making education meaningful in the lives of at-risk kids. There was one reason for this: John Genasci—as gifted a principal as I have known. He convinced Debby and the others to come because he had a dream of a school that could make a difference. She could be on the ground floor and build it with him. That is why so many of the people she started out with became friends: they were change agents, not willing to settle. They wanted to create a school that was synonymous with student success. The beauty of starting fresh is that you don't know what you will lose. This was the best world: create a place where kids loved school.

Lisa was the woman Debby could rely on to be straight with her—in or out of school. She and her partner, Barbara Barnhart, became close with both of us. We listened as she made plans to build her first home—an audacious idea of which Debby and I simply couldn't conceive. She found a design that would insulate it more and reduce the costs of construction. It looked like a wooden Quonset hut but inside it had more room than the average house. It took her almost a year to get it approved and built. Debby and I marveled at her ability to do such things, to step into the unknown and come out with this finished structure.

The best part of living in Washoe Valley was waking to Mt. Rose each morning. Our front window faced west, straight into that mountain rising from the valley floor. We skied there often and somehow managed to believe we had found our new home.

We walked to the end of our dirt road and into the sage at the edge of the lake. Slowly the earth began to pound and dust rose in every direction. Our dog was completely befuddled: hundreds of jackrabbits were running right by us, so fast we did not know what had happened until they were gone. Somehow the dog had spooked them, and like the Washoe before us, flushed them from their dens to run in fear of their lives. Debby was reading *Rabbit Boss* at that time but never imagined she would walk into a scene from the book.

CHAPTER TWO

Waist-Deep in Pyramid Lake

Yesterday, in the waist-deep waters of Pyramid, my rod iced up after every cast. It was twenty-four degrees. Four strikes but no keepers. My neighbor was in a float tube reeling a four-pound cutthroat. He blew the smoke from his mouth, "I'm a dick—haven't gone to see him," the Virginia City High School teacher who was heavy with cancer. This is the work of a small town—the inscrutable roots which reach to encroach on our daily affairs. Even in absence we must pay attention.

Pyramid Lake is almost as large as Lake Tahoe but it couldn't be more different. Thirty miles northeast of Reno, it is a lunar landscape, pristine to the eye, a contrast of water and high desert. Driving over the last ridge to the lake, you know at once you are alone, and necessarily so.

I had not been to Pyramid in a year—when Jess Hayashi was there, fighting the headwinds with a river rod. He had a ladder and enough winter clothes for an arctic expedition but none of it helped. None of it offered so much as a nibble. He was angry at the birds—"worthless coots"—and me, I suspect, for trying to do something like fish in the hard wind. Foolishly, I thought it would make him happy—he an inveterate angler, the kind who fished before eating in any weather or time.

But I was wrong; it was too much like work. We threw all the gear in his '68 Chevy ¾ ton Sub and he cussed all the way home. So much for relief.

Driving out to Pyramid that cold morning I followed the Truckee River north from Wadsworth—through the boxed houses of the Paiute Reservation: poverty, suffering, and isolation—these three from the legacy of our tongues. I stopped at the historic marker sign: Captain Storey was massacred here—the man sent to fight the Paiutes and bring relative peace to the Comstock. A last stand of sorts—not Custer, not close, but good enough for our county's namesake… and why we have to spell Storey with an *e* in perpetuity.

The canyon is small where the attack occurred. Hubris must have been riding a separate horse. If the day was cold, clouded, and the cottonwoods spare, Captain Storey would have presumed a near perfect attack: a surprise in the early light. But like the last nomads of so many valleys in Nevada, the Paiutes were staged and struck before the captain could respond. I have reread the lines from Frank Bergon's novel, *Shoshone Mike*, many times—"Mike did not know where in this country he would ever find a place to live."

*   *   *

The waters of Pyramid are a near-perfect image of Anaho Island to the east, a bird sanctuary for hundreds of white pelicans and other migrating species, the chopped peaks in snow-clouds, and the tidal eddies at my waders. Color comes fresh every morning. I am rarely at peace like this—the water ebbing at my legs, pinching my boots with the pressure below the surface, fingers iced with satisfaction: this is not an ordinary day. Snow flies at my neck; the wind is my companion. Without it, these waters would lie endlessly still.

The ratchet squeals and I yell, something very sweet is on the end of the line—the black and red fly set in the mouth of the fish. I strip the line slow, the rod tip high with tension and turn to face the shore—at least fifty feet, I may not make it. I have no net. I strip him close—maybe twenty feet from my boots. A shake and he is gone. That is why most fly fishermen either love or hate Pyramid. Lahontan cutthroat trout are slow to respond, delirious in the company of humans who pretend to understand the rhythm of this Pleistocene lake.

You can only keep two fish per day over 24 inches or one over 2 feet and one within 17 to 20 inches—big enough to smoke in the snow when everyone else is eating turkey. It was November, after all. My neighbor taught me to fish these waters and it is him I think of whenever something is on or off the line.

I stood against the car in my waders and poured some coffee for my neighbor. I started to think about preparing for my classes at the college the following day. When I mentioned the classes to him, he said he wished he had a job like mine—with meaning. I cautioned him—his work had meaning too—but he felt stagnant, like he wasn't going anywhere. We fished in silence the rest of the day and I walked the shoreline; my waders slowly filled with water.

*   *   *

Captain Storey and his men were ambushed. Could it be any different for us—our people coming west in the shake and rattle of covered wagons? The lake is high in salinity because of the water wars—all the down-streamers who need or want their share. The Truckee River has spilled from Lake Tahoe to Pyramid Lake long before Captain Storey and long before us, its most recent settlers. The region is bound with land-locked lakes that have no outlet, remnants of another era when this place was an ocean floor. Twenty thousand years have passed since then. Does anyone understand the peace of this lake? Foolish of me to ask such a question and foolish of me to want such knowledge. Foolish of me to suppose there are solutions to the history of shared lands. Foolish of me to live my life in a place of such conflicted values—gold and silver plundered for a war of civil rights. If it were only Lincoln and Twain with whom I had to reckon, I would never doubt my decision to come here. But it is so much grayer and the gray becomes diffuse when the particles of light disappear.

Pyramid has never answered my questions except of course, to remain a place of peace, a place where my questions slip away. Although fragile in this time, it is unlike the 1930s when Clark Gable and others came for the record trout until they slowly disappeared. Before that, fishing was the livelihood of the Paiutes for millennia.

I took the Pyramid Highway home to Sparks. I passed the Creel Station, and its sign, "All fisherman must stop, fish or no fish," somehow made the journey worthwhile. It was closed. It was still early in the season. The boat fishermen were dragging lines down about 15 to 20 feet so I was lucky to take one home even though I couldn't show off our catch. The purists insist that catch and release is the order of the day, and for the most part so do I. But I wanted to smoke trout to take the edge off the week ahead.

The highway began to swell with houses, shops and the quick-stop gas stations. I ran in for chips and a granola bar. It would have been cheaper to eat some real food.

At home I gutted the two-pound fish and started the smoker. The wind forced me to the driveway where I was shielded by the fence. I had enough coals for one long smoke. The year before I put the apple stems in a pile by the side of the house. They were dry now and I broke them on the coals to flavor the trout. The trout stretched from one side of the smoker to the other. I wanted take some to the teacher—my neighbor taught him to fish Pyramid too.

The next day he answered the door, frail and unable to see me, his immune system compromised. I handed him the fish and he tried to smile but it was strained. Empty oxygen bottles were on the porch. I left his house unsure of anything. One day when he was fishing at Pyramid, he caught two ten-pounders in a half-hour. Some people fish their whole lives and never see a ten-pound cutthroat. They live in the newspaper—usually a neophyte and sometimes a crusted shore fisherman happily framed with his catch.

Maybe he found his way back to that day when the waters gave him enough. Maybe we will find our way forward now that they no longer do.

Yesterday I was in a Reno fly shop. It's closing; it can't compete with the box stores. I laughed when the young man at the register cajoled me with stories of women trolling for the feathers—to use in their hair, not to tie flies. Twenty-eight years of fly-fishing lore, that means something, almost long enough to see the Truckee River flow year-round into the lake. In drought years it has slowed to a standstill, but through many negotiated agreements, it now runs most of the year, which of course, keeps Pyramid's salinity from rising even further and the cutthroat alive.

Maybe the waters have given us enough to recall *our* time here. Unlike my neighbor and Jess who live to fish, it is the lake's providence that sustains me, when just decades before, that was in doubt. So often the solution is within reach—in this case, keeping this vast body of water alive, and for this brief moment it is alive. That is something to record: a lake has come back from the edge of extinction.

CHAPTER THREE

Braiding the Wind

This is our fourth year of waking to wind. It is 1983 but already I have forgotten when it started. Yesterday, two women visiting the Comstock from the Northwest stopped me on the street: "Does it always blow like this?" they asked with trepidation. I intimated it could. Then they understood: this was something that was required to stay in a place, something unwanted. Her face puckered: "I live in Seattle and the rain…." She didn't need to say more. The wind had burrowed into sleep, into pores, into the sills of home and office.

When Debby and I moved to Virginia City the two of us sat on the porch of our home, the sun having come back at last, and the wind subsided. It blew all night and we felt we had escaped the rhythm of another galaxy. The house shook violently, the windows and doors almost kept the leaves and debris from the hallway. I tried to imagine what it was like a hundred years earlier when insulation was a newspaper in the walls. I wrote her a poem, "All the Worthwhile Things Are in Bed," because I hoped it was a freak occurrence, "… knowing the wind nearly howled/ me to death last night." We had no idea this was the refrain of the high desert, the rule by which you live on the edge of a mountain, atop a canyon of dry land.

In Southern California we had the Santa Ana winds. One night my father and I staked a playhouse he was framing for my sisters. It was nothing more than 2 X 4 framed walls. By morning the walls were twisted to the ground. The wind had bent quarter-inch lag bolts to right angles. It was the wind from the desert. It had blown from the Mojave and over the mountains into our backyard. With it came the threat of fire because Southern California was also dry. It was disquieting, there was nothing to do but wait it out. Sometimes the wind blew for three weeks. My boyhood friend told me of the termination winds in Hanford, Washington, where his father worked in the nuclear plant. The wives huddled in the Quonset huts for weeks on end and then finally, when they could take it no more, left. No amount of money was worth the dirge of wind. I've watched movies of this: it's like they were at the bottom of a giant spinning top, dust everywhere. You could barely make out the structures they lived in.

When the wind starts it is difficult to concentrate on something larger. I awoke at five yesterday, tried to sing myself back to sleep. At the college, our accountant said her husband slept for an hour. The wind sculpts this earth until it finally relents—what grows here grows out of obstinacy: a tree of heaven, a juniper, a locust, and a blade of grass that we persist in tempting for the half-life of summer. Debby plants flowers, bulbs, fruit trees and they dry before the night is over. I water them like they were infants because the wind is an omnivore. It cannot be bothered with what is green or red or purple for the instant of blooming. In the backyard, when the snow dries we try to sit and have friends for a barbeque. We last until the sun goes over Mt. Davidson, triggering a change in atmospheric pressure. The heat from the desert floor rises and soon is pushed back down from the currents overhead. I think the wind must have started in Asia and blown for weeks to get here but in truth, it is just going to work, driving us from our lawn chairs into the safety of the house. If the coals are still flickering I spray them. The yard is little more than leaves and bark and dry grass. Usually the wind stops by the time we turn out the lights. Morning is calm, morning is the time to reflect on the porch when the wind has shaken everything we believe.

Today, it is not that wind. It must be coming from a place far beyond the eye. The sky to the east is reddened with dust. If there is a baseball game this afternoon, it will be hard to see the ball. They will not call the game, not here. It would be like calling the game because of snow in Minnesota. They will taste dust through every inning. They will wear protective clothing. They will shower the grit from their faces.

At work my colleagues are on edge. The windows bow in a bad gust. In Virginia City, a house was blown a foot off the foundation in a bad storm. A house. The roof of the gas station took flight and landed a hundred feet away. Now it is anchored in concrete pillars, three feet in diameter. The wind is a diagram of what is lost. When it blows like this there is nothing to record save its buffeting sound: the clip holding the metal door to the electrical panel has popped again, the lilac groans against the flu pipe, and the shed roof flaps like a dress. It is sheet metal; it makes little difference. On the woodpile there are rocks and timbers, enough weight to hold down a body but in a strong gust, they will fly. The fence will fly with it. New or old, they are sails in the wind. My neighbor's fence lasted less than a month. It is a mark of distinction if your fence is standing at the end of the year. In Houston, they have conversations about how to beat the fire ants. Here, it is how to set a fence post in the wind, how to hang a door so that most of the dust stays outside.

When I first started at the college I needed to make a little extra money in the summer and so I began building fences for friends. My father was still alive and he spent a week helping me set the posts and frame the rectangle of a fence for Debby's colleague at Washoe High School, Lisa Hixson. It was quite enough to cut through the sage; their roots spiraled below the surface. They ruined chainsaw blades. The top six inches of soil were soft, there was little with which to make a hole. I kept digging, down three feet or more. The hole was more than two feet in diameter, a lousy foundation for a fence post. We started at the corners and once the concrete set, put the other posts at six feet intervals until there was an outline with which to begin. I had no idea if it would last through the first gust but I loved the sweat in the sun, the earnest labor with my father, a man who had built many things in the wind.

Six years later, in 1989, when we moved across the street, he helped me frame the floor joists for the bathroom and marveled at setting the roof trusses by hand. Had a wind blown then, my neighbors and I would have flown the eight feet to the ground, the trusses splintered. It took four of us to raise the header over the garage door. We did it on a day without wind. Somehow those days become more important the longer you live here. They are the days of contrast. They are the days when to sit in the sun with stillness is a gift, something remembered but not taken for granted. They return me to the quiet for which I came. They return me to the porch of our first house. They return me to the stump I sat on while I typed my early drafts in the sun, when it was still, and I could hear the breath of my dog. Stillness and wind, these are the two poles with which we live. They form the braid in my hands, the constant of air slipping from this point to that, the thing I try to hold as it disappears.

At Pyramid Lake there is a rock outcropping the Paiutes named Stone Mother, after their story of migration to the lake. She has sat at the water's edge in the wind and sun of a thousand calendars. Her hair and mouth were formed by patience, what is left of the wind and water. One night we slept on the eastern shore, fifty yards from Anaho Island. The wind came up at midnight and I knew the anchor would not keep the boat from shore. Debby climbed in the stern and I pushed hard. I put the canvas over the bow; we were riding straight into the waves. It took an hour to go eight miles. It was black, the marina did not come into view until I saw a truck tire hanging at the inlet. We slept in the boat on the west shore; the stars were something like a cloth of silver. The wind subsided. At dawn we pushed the black sand from our eyes, the lake was peaceful. Nothing was lost.

I wonder what the Stone Mother braids in her hands. I wonder for whom she waits, careful that no distraction interrupts her vision. I wonder if she is braiding a wind from another time, when the lake was at her knees and the light overhead was a constellation of candlelight. Even now, she waits in the wind, exposed like firelight. Her surface is hardened, close to sandstone and the eyes peer across the lake, the lake that every year draws someone to its depths. We have been on the east shore when boats have come in the cove behind Anaho Island and they anchor, thinking the wind is an anomaly, something that will cease in minutes or hours. It only increases and before long, they are trying to save their boats from sinking. It is a lake of tension and peace. Maybe this is what she braids in the wind. Maybe the Stone Mother has seen these extremes for millennia and she can only wait for the time when silence returns.

The wind blows on this mountain to remind us why we ever thought we could live here. It is not howling out of anger, it is howling because we never took it seriously. We thought we could build homes here, grow gardens, make tunnels in the earth, and go about the business of our lives without worry. It is blowing to remind us: we chose this place. The wind kept it from intrusion for thousands of years. Only the migratory hunters came through here, season after season. There was nothing for them save the pine nuts in fall. How could this place possibly hold a community when the wind is its oldest inhabitant?

It is the fourth day of wind and clouds. The fourth day since the beginning of spring. At a friend's yesterday, the fruit trees were starting to bloom and last night a neighbor brought daffodils to dinner. These small reminders, tales from a green land, trick us into thinking we can live in this place. They must be messengers from another locale where there is more water, where there is calm in the skies. They must be the idea of relative ease that we mistake for the ten weeks of summer when the wind blows us from the lake in the afternoons and we retreat to shelter. They must be the twelve days when the wind subsides and we think we have landed in the most beautiful place on earth. We have spent afternoons on Lake Tahoe when no wind blew, when the only ripples were from my feet, when it was so calm I could see the trout below. When it seemed there could be no greater tranquility, we drifted off to sleep and gave thanks. How is it you can live in two places at once, this place of wind and calm? How is it that one can inform the other? I have given up trying to explain the etymology of what I cannot see, this persistent shadow that comes and goes. This wind that turns in and out of me, that becomes a braid of patience, of reluctance to change despite its presence.

My friend, Gary Short, a poet from American Flats, wrote a poem about the wind. There was nothing on the page but the title. The wind had taken it from view. Most people thought it was a printing error, that in the haste of making the book, the poem had been severed from its title. But there was nothing missing; it was written this way, written with the page wide open, nothing to hide, and nothing to declare. Here we are, years later, still trying to make sense of the obvious: where is the poem, why is it missing from the page? I suppose the same could be said of us, of our inexorable desire to calm the wind, the wind that will never be calmed.

It is a particular geography that accounts for the wind and most right-minded people would rather not claim it. They would let the place drift to its own accord, return to what it once was. That's what they tell me when they pass through, when they move from here to there, like the wind, unwilling to touch down, to stay in this expanse. By now we have chosen, we have made up our minds to remain and surrendered any knowledge of permanence. Our story is transitory. We may not be here long. We may disappear like the wooden sidewalks of this town, we may fragment but for now, it is home. It is what we try to imagine as beauty and on the four or five afternoons when the wind dies down, we claim it for our own. We have no one to thank for this gift but our obdurate predecessors; we are free to wander the Virginia Range with the mountain bluebird, the first harbinger of spring.

*   *   *

I was troubled by other decisions I could not attribute to wind. In the four years since we were in Virginia City, Debby and I married and began to make it our home. But I did not know if we could really last in this place. I did not know what it would do to our children when they came. I was afraid to ask the obvious: what if we became disenchanted with this place we chose?

I was beginning to feel stifled at the college and Debby wanted more from her counseling job at the alternative high school. My boss at the college encouraged us to apply to grad school—much as he had done early in his career. Debby got in and so we left Virginia City for Stanford University for four years. It was the biggest challenge of our adult lives: six weeks after arriving Debby gave birth to our first son. I nearly lost them both. She had a placenta previa and the doctors had to cut through the placenta to get him out. For two and-a-half days, we did not name him. We were in shock—what had we done, disrupting our lives like this, moving from our beautiful perch on the edge of a mountain to the tiny confines of married student housing? Finally, we chose the name, Nevada, because it reminded us of our home. I had no insurance, worked two jobs, and tried to keep my wife from going out of her mind while she was confined to bed rest for the first six weeks of her doctoral program. Fortunately, my mother-in-law came to live with us. She took care of Debby and Nevada until Debby could return to her classes.

I finally got a job as a counselor at Stanford so I could see the two of them during the day. I was working with refugees, people with disabilities, and single mothers, all of whom were trying to secure jobs on campus. There were days I came home unable to do anything more than listen to Bob Parlocha on Alameda's legendary jazz station, KJAZ, and drift off to sleep. But I made stellar friends—a Latin-speaking mathematician who was a high school principle in Vietnam and now worked as an account clerk; a social work graduate who would succumb to multiple sclerosis but not before teaching me what it was to be alive every day; a Stanford gymnast who broke his neck and became a preeminent programmer for the university—after nearly two years to convince his superiors that he could work with a twenty-four-hour caregiver; a Nepalese immigrant who took me with him to his village of Pokhara when Debby finished graduate school.

There were other lessons I did not want to learn: when my black boss was repeatedly turned down for promotions or when my immigrant clients were turned away, there was no clear reason. It was just not the right fit. But it could have been any issue really, any issue that no one was willing to talk about: drugs, alcohol, prison. It was fear that turned them away, and fear that kept coworkers from saying more about it. At one point I was so fed up I almost left. I wanted to take Nevada home until Debby finished and just live in peace. I felt caged in the Bay Area but she was adamant that I stay. She felt it would break us in two. She was right.

That's when I left to go see Jess. He lived in Redding, four hours from the university with traffic on a Friday night. I arrived in a stupor and sipped a beer while he promised we would fish the ugliness away. The next morning, after wrangling the gear into the boat, he looked at me and laughed: "What *are* you doing down there? It sounds like…" but I didn't hear the rest of the sentence. What I heard was the solace of a friend who didn't give a shit about my work in the city at a university. What I heard was the water lapping at the aluminum boat and the motor puttering, a stringer of hapless trout staring up at us. What I heard was another man trying to push back his work on Saturday morning. It wasn't that Debby didn't know any of this; she knew it very well. She loved Jess like I did but she knew also that if I got away for an occasional visit, I was a lot happier come Monday.

After I returned from Redding, I took Nevada outside to the lawn in front of our apartment. The grass was high and he pulled away from me. He wanted to walk. His arms spun like blades and suddenly he was upright, as sure as if he were on a wire. I watched him break free of all that had sheltered him, of the tiny threshold that was our apartment. I wrote him a poem, "Watch Him Walk," with the closing lines—"Oh my son, where/ did you learn to walk like that?"

There was wind that morning too. His blond hair was blowing— by then it was in ringlets—and I let go of him, certain that I would have to earn the love of my son. I wanted Nevada to trust that wind like it was his own. I decided right then that nothing was more important than caring for him. I didn't know how I would do that any more than I knew how to live in Nevada when I arrived. I just knew that I had to find a way to be a father wherever I was. By the time we left Stanford, Debby's doctoral program took an extreme toll on her love of learning and we grew more and more convinced that for any real change to take place in the lives of the people with whom we worked, we would have to work for ourselves.

Two years after returning home to Virginia City, we had our second son, Cody, in 1989, and six weeks later, moved across the street. We didn't want to; I had just finished building a garage on the south side of the house. My neighbor made us an offer we couldn't refuse and we were running out of space, so we said yes. Debby ran an educational research center at the University of Nevada, Reno, and I commuted to the Bay Area to coordinate a youth employment program at four universities. It was the first time in my adult life I was able to write in earnest. My consulting job took twenty hours per week and I wrote the rest of the time until my first book came out in 1991: *Desert Wood: An Anthology of Nevada Poets.* Three years later the book of poems I wrote in the evenings at Stanford came out: *Snowmelt.* The title poem came from one of those life-saving trips to visit Jess.

That the wind returns is our constant. My boys are defined by it; Debby cusses it like a relative who won't go. We take time out from its persistent calling to rebuild what it has taken down. It is what we know of living on a mountain. If it relents, it is our thread to the next day. It snowed all night and the wind tore at the eaves and yet I wake to this: a blue horizon of white ridges—snow as far as I can see. Calm, undisturbed quiet.

This is the refrain I hear: *this is why I came*—to know that something beautiful is a footstep away. And today it is.

CHAPTER FOUR

The Trail to Hobart Reservoir

Jess and I pulled our bikes from the car at the trailhead above Carson City. Five miles later I was at Red House, almost to Hobart Reservoir. I looked down the trail to find Jess slowing and out of breath. It was August, 1990. This was not the Jess I knew: a fierce competitor, an athlete. He had finally relented to my pleas and joined me on my annual pilgrimage to Hobart Lake. This lake held special meaning for Nevada and me: we fished and swam and sometimes took Oreo, our Dalmatian, with us up the six miles to the reservoir, 1,700' above the valley floor (Cody was too young to make the trek).

The outlet stream that rushed at our feet was the local engineering feat of the late 1800s: a progressively smaller series of pipes that built enough pressure to sustain a constant water flow down the eastern Sierra and up Jumbo Grade to the Comstock. That system is still in use to this day.

August is dry in the Sierra Nevada. The mule's ears had begun to curl, the woolly mulleins were turning to flower and lupine was almost blown from its stems. This ridge holds many small lakes:

Hobart is the dammed reservoir below Marlette Lake. Both bodies of water were created to transport wood and water to the Comstock. There are native trout in Marlette and until recently, only original landowners could access it to fish. Monique Laxalt has written of the many trips into the lake with her family. Her grandfather, Dominique, was the subject of her father Robert's finest book: *Sweet Promised Land*, which begins with the iambic line, "My father was a sheepherder, and his home was the hills." When I walked among the aspens and Jeffrey pines I thought of him, a hundred years earlier, sitting by himself with sheep, a fire, and his family below in the Carson boarding house.

Jess and I pushed on up the hill, sweat in our eyes. The heat kept the insects down. I threw stream water on my face and wondered how much longer it would be until we could put our bikes down and dive in the lake. I arrived first and found a peanut butter sandwich and an apple in the saddlebag. I unpacked the rod and tied a single, barbless fly on the leader. We always said we caught something, and nearly always lied about the size of the fish when we got home. Jess pulled in ten minutes later. His face was flush, he was out of air. I registered this but didn't pay much attention once we were fishing. The shadows started on the east shore of the lake and we wound our way along its border, hoping the one docile trout would snap the fly. In this rivalry I was never Jess's equal: Jess caught fish as if he were in the water helping guide the trout to the hook. It didn't matter what body of water; he held sway. When I did catch something it was cause for screaming and Jess, of course, thought this ridiculous. He never understood the commotion; fishing was a process—once you mastered it you could repeat it with accuracy and results. He lacked the usual gadgets on his boat—fish finder, nets, endless supplies of line, leaders, tackle, and multiple guides for complete precision at various depths. Fishing was an art and he took it quite seriously. When he took it too seriously, I teased him—because we had come from jobs that, if not serious, were precise in their rules, and we needed to relax. This was the prescription for fishing. Catching was extra, not necessary but part of the myth we made of our journeys into the Sierra Nevada.

       *   *   *

When Jess and I were still in Southern California we worked at a non-profit youth organization in the mid-1970s. One summer he asked if I would join him on a backpack trip into the Sierra Nevada—with the teenagers from the non-profit.

Jess never imagined we would fail: ten recalcitrant kids, a topography map, and me—the gangly ne'er-do-well who went along for the ride. How could he know it would be any different? He had supreme confidence in everything he did. Seven days in the upper Sierra with some water, dried food, and enough rods for a good fish story. Going over Army Pass at 12,000 feet, the July heat was like flame at our faces. We were above the tree line and had to reach the summit and get back down to the campsite before dark. I thought we would until one freckled girl turned the color of a plum and began to see stars. There was no place to hide, no wind, and it was midday. We held a rain poncho over her head, poured water on her, and put a wet rag on her neck. She had heatstroke. Jess and I looked at each other: who would carry her down? I was in putrid shape, and Jess was a braided mass of muscle. It made no difference; we had to get her temperature down. We were at least two days from the trailhead. I don't know who would have lost the coin toss to carry her out, but after a half-hour she began to breathe with more regularity and her natural color was coming back. I said some evil curse to the valley below and we started up again. He pulled out the topo. I asked what the thin lines meant: the lines were closest at the steepest elevations. He was certain we could reach the campsite by dark. The kids whined and the freckled one looked faint but kept hiking.

Finally, the cover of trees, and as sure as the moon, a creek beneath. We made mac and cheese, hung our tube tents and told the kids to gather firewood. This was their third day without cigarettes. They were fidgeting and the altitude made them light-headed. Jess stepped out on the ridge, adjusted his telephoto lens and took shot after shot. He wanted to capture the riverbed below. This was his first time on this route. He had planned the hike for weeks and somehow, we had corralled the kids, driven up Highway 395 to the Lone Pine Trailhead and begun as if it were an idle undertaking. I think Jess worried more about me than them: would I succumb to the weight in my pack, the new boots on my feet, or the unrelenting pining of adolescents?

Two days after that we were on our stomachs in the middle of a long valley at 10,000 feet. The grass was high and there were clouds overhead. He knew golden trout were here, natives, and if we found them it would be worth staying an extra day. How, I asked, could he be sure? The terrible knowing eyes came back to me: this is where they *should* be. The drainage goes to here, he gestured, pointing to the exact place on the topo. Before long, the tiny apparitions appeared: the golden skin with the red stripe. They were hungry, jumping at the shadows. We could not see them, only feel a bump when they hit the fly, and then we lifted the rods sixteen inches to look at their beauty. I had never fished like this, face to the ground, poking my rod over the creek bed. We must have released twenty fish when a voice came from my feet: "Let me see your license," the Fish and Game warden, determined to give us a ticket. How in the hell did he find us—five days out, thirty miles from the trailhead—and beaming in his officious manner? We had more rods than people, a big problem, until we told him there were others at the campsite. He didn't believe us and so we gave up that beautiful tug on the line to walk to the site with our friend. At camp he perused the faces like they were criminals and when he couldn't find a problem, told us to "Watch it," as he hiked away, content to disturb our little nest.

Jess had fifty pounds in his pack, his camera was at least five of those pounds, and could, I imagine, have hiked another week without a whimper. I could barely shoulder forty, but I did and it pissed him off—the sluggard dragging up the single file of adolescent feet. His father hiked the John Muir Trail in twenty-one days, more than two hundred miles. In this we shared our sudden fear: we would never live up to our engineer fathers who pushed and pushed to reach that melancholy jewel, success. Jess was smart but understood that with success came compromise, and could not find it in himself to surrender to such an ideal.

There we were, running from our fathers, high in the Sierra with ten kids, trying to teach them there was more to life than getting stoned. Remarkably, it worked most of the time. Once they got out of the city and filled their lungs with the thin air, the stars overhead were like candles. "Soft science," he used to say, "my dad thinks this is soft science." As if hard science were shorthand for real effort. Still, it didn't matter. The paths we chose made us and broke us down, just like them. But how could we say that at twenty-one? We barely knew our own names, strangely hewn from separate countries, Japan and Ireland. This flesh of ours given to helping others when all our fathers wanted were sons like them.

Sometimes this soft science kept us up all night and the pain of others was soft like blood running from the mouth.

*   *   *

When I finished graduate school at Cal State Fullerton in 1978, I left for a life outside the city. I taught at the college in Yerington. Jess and three others from our non-profit started an alternative school near Redding for those same recalcitrant youth. I called him from my rented house when I lived in that farming valley. The year of our leaving Southern California became a crucial decision in the distance. When he spoke on the phone it was like he was in another country: a crackling line and muted conversation. He had scarce resources and was endlessly tired. It was hard to find the right mixture of out-of-district placements, quality staff, and income to keep the school afloat. An ideal had become a business: something neither of us planned on running. At the time, when I worked for the college, I thought he took a risk, an investment in something imagined. His colleagues were talented with these youth but it was extremely difficult to find the door into a rural community and establish credibility where so many had failed.

At night, when I usually called, his voice was thinned by days of long labor because he was the only mechanical one among his peers. He built most of the structures that were needed: corral, outbuildings, plumbing and wiring for the school buildings, and most incredibly, a bridge to cross the river in and out of the canyon. The latter could have stumped most civil engineers but Jess, having an uncanny ability to find solutions to physical problems, strode on.

In his methodical way, he went to the library, read about bridge span, projected weight balance, required engineering, and tried to convince the building department flatheads what this meant. "Do you have a license to build such structures?" they retorted, and the bluster continued long into the fall. Jess contended he did not need one; he was simply repairing it. The bridge had washed out and this kept both kids and staff from getting to the school. The school staff thought, for a minute, about hiring a contractor, but quickly abandoned the idea when they learned it would cost upwards of $50,000. They were lucky to make payroll so Jess kept at it. I intimated that this might be too much of a project but he insisted there was a way.

Jess's third winter was especially hard. Debby and I had moved to Virginia City. It was 1980 and I was worried about my friend. I called more frequently because it grew harder and harder to keep the school in the black. A chiropractor from Sacramento moved in with Jess. He had a small practice and kept some of the bills off the counter of their doublewide. When Debby and I visited, the trailer was chaotic. Jess left everything in view: fishing weeklies, tackle, oars, rods, batteries, lock boxes, guns, jackets, goggles, chainsaw, and PVC in a literal cobweb of nylon line and dust. I opened the door to the extra bath and the toilet oozed with urine. Coming to clean became a semi-annual retreat for Debby and me. Once, I drove up to find a garden with drip systems, hay bales and trellises. Some order had come into his life. He had met a woman. This was rare in that tangle of redneck northern California. It was the most special gift of that place—local friendship—people with whom he could relate. As taciturn as he was, he drew characters into his orbit and that almost made the sacrifice at the school tolerable.

Big Joe logged during the winters, fished and fixed chainsaws in the off-season. He gave Jess more shit than Merle Haggard gave "them hippies," which Joe delighted in reporting because the country star called Redding home. But underneath Joe's ranting, he cared deeply for Jess. Cutting wood was the one thing he could do with ease—hoisting a twenty-five-inch bar into the green wood made him happy. He had enough sense to find a crew he could trust to fell trees, whether in the rain or on the steep cliffs of the Trinity Alps. His wife worked at the school and kept their three kids loved and fed. It was his body he needed most—strength, supple hands, and sight. To hear the unexpected snap or twist was a daily ritual: pay attention, stay alive. Loggers have few rivals in labor save miners and high-rise steel men. They have the focus of a surgeon, the rhythm of a dancer. When they lose their focus, they must leave or live with the consequences.

Jess took me to Joe's house. His hands were deep-boned mitts, gnarled with grease, calluses, and cuts but he was ready to fish and the more we drank, the better it got. Jess tied my stringer to the edge of the boat and it swung idly in the water, the trout eyes staring up at me. The outboard puttered across Whiskey Town and for an instant I thought we might catch our limit. Joe was pissed he hadn't caught the biggest trout and Jess teased, "You may as well put your rod away."

"Chump," Joe shot back. I laughed, having heard the endless ridicule on the phone, in the doublewide, and beyond. Joe would never say he needed the fish but in the off-season loggers were poor and he had kids in school. His wife worked in the cafeteria and did what she could to make ends meet in the house. She knew he felled trees large enough to bury houses and that counted for something. Most men couldn't try—it spooked Jess when he had to fell a tree at the school. If it spun or splintered, you had a millisecond to move, and if you didn't choose well, it was an arm or leg or worse. Joe had all ten digits and both eyes intact. He might make it till forty—what happened after that he'd let happen. This, too, drew Jess: Joe's particular consciousness that lived in the wild of every day, that built a reason to break off something large and wrestle it to the ground and later, take satisfaction in seeing the job done. "Something no desk could offer," that's what Joe said, stinking up the cab. His truck barely fit the three of us but the bed was stacked with sawhorses and so we made do.

*　　　　　*　　　　　*

Debby and I came to visit in the fall of 1982. The three of us drove to the outlet of Lewiston Dam. It was that thick time when the oaks were brown and the cheat grass was knee-high, the digger pines limp in the heat. It was a long single lane to the mouth of the river. The salmon had returned to spawn. We put our hands in the river and it was frigid. The salmon were discolored and sloughed their skin. Some didn't make it—found the river stones, deposited their roe and floated into our hands. Most of the salmon died at the headwaters where the Fish and Game warden handed them out like turkeys. I looked at the line of people, nearly every person from the hills, and a few, in their Cadillacs, were from the houses on the river. Most were like the Joads and we, too, were in the dusty line. This was our own little trip west looking for food. Doubtless they felt shamed by the feel of fish not properly caught, "…but they were gonna' die anyway," the eighteen-year-old protested. "Yep," I offered, grateful for fresh salmon even though it was too easy, unearned in an essential way. Jess needed the fish to eat that winter and yet, it was an awkward visit with hunger. Most in that line *needed* the fish, the occasion of spawning was a diversion. The fish that sailed up the ladders to meet our hands were the strong ones but today, it was like a picnic of salmon. The river of redress for my friends.

*　　　　　*　　　　　*

Jess threw manzanita in the wood stove until the flue pipe glowed red. He had three extinguishers in the front room of the trailer. Like cottonwood I thought: cheap and easy heat, burns quick and hot. He had no money for wood, even the snags at the school had to be felled and split which took gas and time. There was a protracted silence: "Not well," when I asked how he was doing. He was hunting squirrel, rabbit, what most regard as vermin. "Can I get you something?" His pride choked off any response. "I'll call Joe," I joked, like a visit would change anything.

His chiropractor roommate leafed through cheap porn, the Grateful Dead oozed from the speakers on orange crates, and I sat in the easy chair, exhausted from the drive. Debby, Nevada, and I had returned from Stanford and I needed to see my friend.

Fishing was an excuse to be together. I never took it seriously, any more than I took eating seriously. Fishing was a pastime to be alone with our thoughts in his aluminum boat. I told him to come to the Comstock or Tahoe, to any school nearby. Let the damn place go, he didn't need the persistent headache of paying himself last. They had a reputation: good teachers, strong district liaisons, and a somewhat consistent cash flow, but never enough for the owners. His family helped, and he, ever the willing volunteer, worked harder, longer, until I think it made him wish for a miracle of resignation, a reason to walk away.

Despite the mounting debt, he seemed at home in the dry, northern landscape where everything involved survival. He told me of a woman who lived with her two children in the mountains for seven years, hunted those same rodents, trapped larger game, shot deer in the off season, and canned what vegetables she could grow.

He was certain things would turn around. "Perhaps," I sighed and opened our first beer of the day. He took me to Shasta, the many-fingered lake of houseboats and weekenders from the valley. Joe had a boat with twin Evinrudes, probably from the year of my birth. If I were Catholic I would have crossed myself. At least when the first engine failed the second was sure to start. That was the logic—to be tested by the serene waters of the reservoir. Jess's aluminum boat wouldn't hold all of our gear. I imagined it in a dry dock of oak leaves and fallen Manzanita but we trolled on, the small mouth bass inches below the hook on Joe's fish finder.

Jess knew about the physical world: the fact of its existence was discernible and concrete. His tolerance for the spiritual one, as Debby often said, was limited. I was the anomaly in his universe, a ring around the only place he knew: the quantifiable globe and yet, the disparity between us was unimportant. There were times it had great value: I could not *do* most of the things he took for granted and then, when the subject of poetry came up, he deferred. He understood more would come from that well, implying that art, like his work, emanated from the weight of a similar struggle.

CHAPTER FIVE

Building Community in the High Desert

In 1991, Debby and I started Community Chest, a non-profit organization dedicated to building a healthy community—*our* healthy community. We reasoned we could earn enough money to stay in business if we really worked for the coming year. We rented an office in a chartreuse jewelry store on Virginia City's main street and almost thought we were happy. I remember reading the poet Kenneth Koch's book on teaching children to write poetry, *Wishes, Lies, and Dreams*. I'm not sure which of the three we believed more but off we went.

We started our non-profit to build a lighthouse for children and families—and it is strange that a water image should describe our early efforts at social change. But in truth, there were few examples, little to rely on and certainly no safe passage for what we wanted to do.

This work of social change has its rewards. If you are lucky, people return to tell you about their lives, what has taken place to restore hope, or the outlines of their journeys. You may recall the lineament of their faces.

And it has its frictions. We move slowly and the lasting results, are likewise slow to achieve. Which is fine, unless you are fundamentally flawed by impatience—and we are. We both wanted to do things quickly, turn this dream of serving children and families into reality.

It didn't happen quickly and it didn't happen like we imagined. We were in our 30s, naïve, headstrong, and emboldened with the accidents of our brief lives. Debby gave up her job at the university and I quit my consulting job to direct Nevada's Homeless Youth Education program. It was our first and only grant. All that we knew was what not to do and the ruminations of what would come were hidden from view.

We borrowed a table and two chairs. We hooked up an extra phone from the house and put a sign on the rented office building, Community Chest, Inc. Nothing could stop us now. It took me one year to get our non-profit status, a moral victory given the tendrils of the IRS. Debby quickly wrote a grant for three Volunteers in Service to America, women who organized a food closet, thrift store, and childcare—all available through bartering labor for goods. She then designed a door-to-door survey to determine the human service needs of the county. Over the course of two such surveys in five years, the residents of Storey County said they wanted a youth and community resource center, above all else. This led us to believe, of course, that we could do this—we being five young people, an architect, and Debby and I.

Yet there was no simple way forward. I had never raised large sums of money and did not have any concept of commercial construction. Art Hannifan, our architect, came to the high school to sketch a picture of this ideal place: a building for the itinerant non-profits, childcare, youth programs, health center, and an arts center for the community. In short, a dream hung on the hopes of these young people. Perhaps that is why we plunged ahead. To surrender before starting would have sentenced us, but more important, the young people, to almost certain failure at the real risk—not trying.

I knew a woman through my homeless youth education work that was now in Senator Harry Reid's office. I called and asked for her help. She said to send something along. I drafted some notes and put them in the mail. Of course, they were incomplete: how could I understand what building a community center meant?

In the interim, I woke up one day to find twelve crying infants in my house—nearly stepped on one trying to negotiate passage to the bathroom. It brought back visions of when I met Debby: she ran a preschool in Southern California. I hid from them when I visited: "Miss Debby Loesch, there's a man in the bathroom and he won't come out." This must have been practice for what was to come.

Few of us get time to prepare for such change, much less instruction to do so. Our children needed childcare, as did the children of thirty other parents. We lived on the side of a mountain. To drive up and down it for work was quite enough. To find adequate childcare was too much for most of us. And so—yes, you know what we did.

We parents spent many weekends refurbishing a house so that I could walk through my own place of residence without worry of crunching a Sippy cup.

That childcare center ran independently for ten years before the entropy of finance—low pay for staff, difficult if rewarding work, and bills that left the ledger at zero—brought it to a close.

This was a lesson in business survival—the ability to navigate personnel, payroll, and community with success. Road maps we had not yet read.

Most people do not connote Virginia City with poverty or hunger. It is closer in the public imagination to a *Bonanza* rerun than any still life of public need. Nonetheless, when we opened Community Chest something very unexpected happened: we were asked to address these very issues. At that time Storey County had a population of approximately 4,000, a third of which were low-to-moderate income. Approximately a fourth of the elementary school students participated in the federal free and reduced lunch program before it was curtailed. Employment was limited to tourism unless you commuted off the mountain to Reno or Carson. This necessitated transportation.

Approximately another third of the population were seniors (and still are). Their resources were similarly limited by their fixed incomes. This led us to establish a senior food commodities program. In a very short time, one issue led to the next—counseling, domestic violence, employment, early childhood education, services for at-risk youth, health care, and more. It became increasingly apparent that the need for human services had largely gone unnoticed but now that we had opened our doors, the flood of requests began. Most of the people we served had roots here. In the case of families, if it was a single parent household this meant the parent had to work. Consequently, an affordable after-school program became a necessity. This was the bridge to serving the youth in those families, the bridge into the schools.

Without fully understanding the genesis of rural poverty, this led us to work with our partners in the region to ameliorate these many tough issues. I think it also helped us to put a name on the invisible source of these requests: the stigma of poverty's shame, a difficult subject and in a small mining town, one that is mostly ignored.

*   *   *

I was sitting in a school board meeting when my neighbor (who sold us the house across the street) came flying over my shoulder to say in a few kind words that we were being screwed. A town elder joined him. Something I never thought I'd live to see. This was because we had offended one too many people while running an after-school program, or so it seemed.

Politics are never strange to small towns. The same is true of non-profit work in them. One must be part pacifist and part realist to succeed, or as I would learn, to last. My work with homeless youth had spilled over into our school. I was asked to present to a group of eighth graders, one of whom had lost her home to fire. I explained that being without shelter affected people everywhere and now, it left some in this classroom without a place to live. But there were those who wanted nothing to do with such a discussion. Soon the memos were sent home and the reasons clear: this was not part of the curriculum. I heard it often from the same small group: "I will not permit my child to listen to any discussion of homeless youth." Although it was federal law: homeless children must be admitted to school, it made little difference to the hecklers.

What was clear was the fear of the unknown that it generated. Fear of what poverty represented and fear of finding oneself there. I had always assumed that people wanted the basic tenets of being on this earth—food, shelter, safety, education, and that extended to people without those very things. A restaurateur in San Francisco told me that he grew so tired of watching people dive in his dumpster he locked it. Diving for food. "What we need is a human contract. All people on earth must have the basic resources," he said. He put a face on poverty.

Of course, this was not San Francisco: there were no masks to hide behind. You were either with us or against us. On a good day I tore down two or three ugly letters in the post office. On a bad, our staff would ask me if I had read what they wrote in the newspaper and beyond—to the same senator we had asked for help with the center.

The issue finally landed with the school board, which was an irritant to some and a stage for others: state's righters, religious do-gooders, and sovereign thinkers. When one of the latter, who became a commissioner and a good friend, asked his colleague if *he* wanted to run the after-school program, he declined on behalf of the board. The battle to charge us to use the public space in the school to provide the program ended. But not the ongoing hate mail to our funders, politicians, and the press: "Your wife is vulgar. She steals money from the government. She makes hundreds of thousands of dollars." On and on. Some days it made me puke and I wanted retribution. Somehow if we took federal money, we were bad or certainly capable of being bad. Better to let people suffer the indignity of poverty than to find a way to resolution—even if it was in our small town.

Freedom of the press is not free—unless you are willing to take someone to civil trial for slander and win. These constant attacks hurt many people with whom I worked and lived. At some point Debby and I chose to move through the confusion of work that was much larger than any of us while still not knowing if something would come of it.

Somewhere in the smoke of those days we held countless meetings in our house to find people to run for the school board. People were afraid to run for office, afraid of threatening the status quo and living with the consequences of that decision. This became a recurring theme in our work. I remember a founding board member telling me of change: people were more afraid of what they had to give up than they would get. As good a definition as any and one that only grew more complex as we continued.

People were afraid to take a stance because of the stigma associated with it. We were outsiders trying to provide programs for youth in the schools but a few religious zealots painted our work as being a blemish on the community. "We don't have poor people here; we have all the resources we need. Don't tell us how to run our lives, much less our children's lives. My child won't be exposed to such people. How dare you bring the needs of *those people* into the classroom." A familiar refrain: keep poverty at a distance and it goes away.

None of this was civil rights legislation or work that required great personal risk. It was subtler—learning to find partners in the nuanced world of local politics, leaders and elders who ran things after the election. In other words, we made a daily effort to be the same person at the post office, the garage, and the basketball game. We had to earn the respect of those who lived here and belonged to this community. We were outsiders and to make matters worse, wanted to change how things had been done for decades. Of course there was resistance but there was also a great need. To ignore it would mean we would have to leave. We chose to stay, partly because of the beauty I alluded to and partly because it was the logical extension of our lifework. All the risk we had taken to this point— leaving my tenured job at the college, going to grad school when Debby was pregnant, working with non-profits as an advocate— had led us to this place in time. Debby's graduate work was in child development and evaluation—she knew about families and children. I had worked with youth for most of my adult years and I saw in systems, particularly large ones, an inability to thrive, to be resilient, to respond to the needs of their constituents. This was simply one more step into the unknown but it would test us to our bone-depths.

We knew very few people and we were miles from the center of political influence in this community but our non-profit work brought us closer to its hub and demanded that we participate. This was the rub: if you wanted to change anything you had to risk being disliked, and simultaneously, build relationships that made this change possible.

*   *   *

When I started the statewide homeless youth education program my former boss at the college told me "there were so few funds," you could not make a difference. I soon learned that what made a difference was not money, but guts—being able to find a way into the room and discuss the very thorny issue of being without shelter. For most of us, it has no tangible consequences in our lives.

This is further exacerbated by the material wealth in our country: how can there be poor people; my life is fine or passable. Those people, a killing phrase that later titled one of my poems, were invisible and so to talk about such issues, particularly in regards to public education i.e., access to school, adequate food in school, adequate study areas after school, access to clothes and transportation, meant that things had to change. Most of all, it meant we had to change how we thought about education when it was secondary to the hunger experienced by the child being taught.

Unbeknownst to me, this was the greatest lesson I could be given. Without having an adequate answer to the fear that this issue raised in most people, I had to learn what it meant so that I could assuage their concerns and move beyond fear to tolerance. This became the standard for much of the work that would ensue at Community Chest: to develop a keen understanding of the issue and an even stronger ability to state it in non-threatening terms, forge critical alliances with people on all sides of the question and finally, implement a solution that was right. Frequently this took years to understand and put into practice. This is what they do not teach in college: the layering of knowledge upon calculated risk to develop solutions to extremely complex social problems. Even knowing this was minimally important. Without a critical mass and long-term commitment on behalf of a few, this knowledge did little to change systems.

We had to learn something else: poverty is inextricably linked to the systems which maintain it. What's worse, some profit from those very systems. Without trying to untangle them, without trying to reach a new threshold of what was expected for daily living, we changed very little. Indeed, we simply maintained the systems that perpetuated poverty. This is radical information and yet, it is older than the Bible. It is our inability to recognize the charity model as debilitating that keeps us from looking for real solutions. For that model to change, we must also change. For me, it comes down to how you treat people: if I cannot countenance hunger in my family, it cannot exist elsewhere. We've had the tools to end hunger for a century. It is not a priority. The same could be said of shelter and most diseases. It does not mean, however, we cannot try to find a new paradigm for living equitably.

I grew increasingly tired of watching people's eye close when I spoke. I asked my younger son, Cody, if I could use his picture on a poster. It read: No Child Deserves to Be Hungry. Exploiting a homeless child for this purpose was wrong. It may have been wrong to put my own son's picture on the poster. But people got it: a child does not ask to be hungry. They do not understand its consequences and its antecedents. We do. We can do better.

Later, in a similar moment of frustration, I made a new poster for a billboard in Las Vegas. It read: There Are No Homeless Children in Nevada. At the bottom it said, Learn about the Problem, Get Involved, Volunteer. The outrage was immediate: how could I make such a statement? What was I thinking? How dare I say something so outlandish? Of course it was my colleagues in the charity business who were most frustrated. As long as there were bread lines, there would be jobs for us.

This has been stated by a hundred people much smarter than I, and yet we persist in believing otherwise, even when the folly of our actions are repeated: more than one hundred years ago, Francis Perkins wrote as much for her thesis when she graduated from Columbia with her master's degree in political science:

"…temporary relief is necessary, and its method may well deserve discussion, but it is after all only an expedient to head off malnutrition until society adjusts itself and provides adequate incomes and adequate education to all its workers." (Karenna Gore Schiff: *Lighting the Way: Nine Women Who Shaped Modern America*).

Something very unusual happens when you start a small business: people ask you to do other things. As I said, there was no human service infrastructure in Storey County. Almost overnight, people came to us to ask if we could address more youth and family issues. We grew rapidly and still, we did not understand what we were about to undertake. In four years we outgrew our rented space and found a building to buy. Again, there was no money and banks ran when they saw us. The parents of our baby sitter offered to carry the loan (it was their building), with the caveat that we pay it off in four years. We swallowed hard, spent $50,000 to bring the building up to code and moved in. It took me one year to find a bank that would agree to loan us the money—as long as we put our house up for collateral. That was in 1995.

The finer points of non-profit management: we promptly left for Chile.

Another lesson: trust those you work with to reach much farther than you ever imagined.

The building was empty, the furniture scattered in sheds, the computing and phone systems still unsolved. It was a three-story Victorian and the heaviest desk, mine, had to climb a Harry Potter stairwell. We almost stayed but realized that to do so was unwise: we needed to rest so that we could continue, so that we could last.

We returned refreshed to a fully furnished office and a very proud team.

CHAPTER SIX

Learning from the Artists

It is 1996 and we are in our new building. We are hopeful, and we believe that the business may survive. We have a staff of six. We have learned how to do payroll, insurance, audits, and loans. We have poured eight-foot concrete footings, floated driveway cement and prayed the carpet installer will not kill the electrician. And still—.

I have just come from the painter, Jeff Nicholson's, gallery. His new oil is on the wall: *Evening Shadows Across Nevada.* It is a silted light weaving from range to range, slowly disappearing in the east, until finally the sage and occasional piñon are lost like a compass bearing. It is a near-perfect representation of the landscape, but it haunts with what is not there: an ease, a sense of permission to go about one's business. This could not be truer of social change. The oldest metaphor—social change is glacial—might be a foundation, but in Nevada it is cumulative—embedded in rock, canyons, history, and mines: our work has taken five years and we have only begun.

I left Jeff's gallery looking at that painting, looking at his thin frame, thinking of the three months it was on the easel, trying to reconcile a life spent in the creation of art and a life spent in the creation of social justice. Are they disparate, do they have some common thread, some unifying force? An artist tempts the lonely beadwork of survival. They are rarely free of its collar. To paint without fear of reprisal, one must find redress in solitude, perfect the image that emanates from the imagination. In this, we have much in common: there is little to rely on when you start a non-profit, except faith in an image found only in the imagined world of a just globe. We, too, were never far from the beadwork of survival. We had to choose how this image would be represented, how our work would manifest itself. The same could be said for all people who take care to make their vision real—whether scientist or florist, the dance of practice, repeated attempts at success or some part of it, that is the process. In the case of social change this meant there was still more to do: negotiate a path forward when the stakes were highest.

Jeff's example helped me find my way forward: as a poet I could not work in isolation, could not afford to stay home and write. I didn't want to—I had a responsibility to this community, to this effort to build it but I could not forsake my poetry; it kept me alive. Most days, if I did nothing else, writing a poem was lifesaving. The poems began to be diagrams of the journey Debby and I undertook—even when the diagrams went nowhere.

I awoke this morning and told Debby I was flattened. The inexorable push to finish the center was making its presence felt. Negotiating with foundations, builders, inspectors, tenants and more, finding the isolated truth hidden in a comet of budget cuts, economic downturns, and failed promises. Debby and I never imagined any of this when we began to design the community center in 1996 with five young people and Art, the architect. That's why time is so integral to our survival: there is a history of countless struggles, not unlike ours. We fell to our knees to learn once again, humility to start anew. Our nascent strength grew from that core—almost like painting without fear of reprisal.

A former foundation director called this morning: he is running a 5K race and wants to donate his proceeds to Community Chest—along with a legislator who had heard my testimony in front of numerous committees. Slowly the web arcs to a close: I asked the five youth to testify in the Assembly Chambers on behalf of the center. One by one they came up to the microphone. The Chairman, the late Assembly Speaker Joe Dini from Yerington, had introduced a bill to fund, in part, the construction of the center. He did not know if it would make it through committee but encouraged us to go through the process. I simply wanted the young people to learn what participatory democracy meant, to have a stake in the outcome of their building, their future. Speaker Dini welcomed them, made them feel like it was their building and their rightful place at the podium.

The young people who testified that day were turned down—there was not enough money to pass the bill. But they learned why their voice was necessary in the public dialogue: without it, others made the rules.

*   *   *

I thought of Karen Kreyeski, the Silver City painter who taught English and art at Virginia City High School but found a way to keep painting. I was so taken with her watercolors I asked if she would consider painting the cover art for my first book of poems, *Snowmelt*. To my surprise she said yes. Not only did she paint the cover art—which hangs in our living room to this day—she painted two more watercolors that preface the other sections in the book. The visual images were crisp and sensual. She made this landscape appear as if it were a human figure, a woman's torso entwined in the snowmelt. The moon was a pale purple, rising in the half-light of dusk. The flanks of the mountains were blue and flecked with red watercolor pencil. She rendered the place of my awakening for the cover of this book. It set the poems in a physical context of subtle beauty, what I hoped to see every morning.

The way she worked—after school, at night, on the weekends—also told me I could do so. I could make poetry in between the layers of my life at Community Chest. As improbable as this seemed my work also gave me an anchor: there was something to write about, just as her teaching gave her a depth of feeling that she brought to her painting. Those images are a constant reminder: without art, I become sterile, lost in the deadlines of grants and minutia. I turn to that painting daily for perspective, for resolve.

I continued to send out requests for the center. My friend in Senator Reid's office had asked him to sponsor a bill on behalf of the project. I called every month, sent e-mails and waited. I was assured it was being reviewed and in a few months I would hear something.

Art worked on the plans and incorporated most of what the public and youth desired. They wanted to build a facility that would cover the adjacent pool and house all of the youth and family activities. That was in the three-million range, a figure that seemed unreal. A number with no antecedent and yet the costs to keep the office running were steadily building. I had little choice but to put the project on the back burner until I could navigate the immediate fiscal uncertainty in the office.

*   *   *

Tom Gilbertson is a big man, a Vietnam Vet, who opened an art gallery in the early 1990s. A painter, he was determined to make Sun Mountain Artworks last on the Comstock. I spent many afternoons in his shop talking about poetry, painting, and our friends who were artists. This excerpt is from his essay on his painting gathered in a book of art by Vietnam vets (*Vietnam: Reflexes and Reflections*, edited by Eve Sinaiko): "Sometimes, as I drive through a barren mountain pass in Nevada, when it's drizzling rain and the light is just so, I am surprised not to see a bunker, swathed in barbed wire, looming from the crest of the hill…." He was building a community of artists—people who exhibited in his gallery and who turned to him for framing. He taught art part-time and worked as an artist in residence to subsidize the gallery.

Tom helped me understand what building a community meant: it was about relationships, about tending to the routines in people's lives. He taught me how to make a place for art in a community and how a man could change his community with art. He encouraged my meager attempts at writing poetry and was particularly interested in my poetry workshop at the prison. I started teaching the workshop in 1989. Some of the men were also painters and Tom expressed interest in holding a show of their art. When I published the journal of their poetry, *Razor Wire*, Tom hosted an art and poetry opening—a first for the men in the workshop and for Tom. Tom showed me that art, like our work, could make a difference.

Social change is not required to stay alive—like food or shelter. When there is money everything seems possible. We can talk about building a culture that thrives, a community that prizes its young people, a society that is, indeed, civil. When it disappears, you must find a way to go on whether or not there is money, just like an artist. Staff must be paid, the building must be repaired and the hard tools of this profession—discourse, compromise, and vigilance—tarry in the dust.

To my eternal embarrassment and chagrin, I could not stop the bleeding. I took on extra work, donated all of the money to the office to have a cushion for payroll. I wrote poems about making payroll and tried to find a way to finish the biweekly cycle without giving my own money back. I didn't want to share this, I think Debby knew and maybe a few others but felt it was my responsibility to resolve what is, for most small businesses, the crucible of success: cash flow. This business is retroactive—we bill for work already done and it takes weeks, months to receive those payments. In the interim, I carried up to $50,000 and called and wrote and pleaded with accountants to follow through on our requests for payment. We had no credit—the business was month-to-month and a bank may as well have been in another country, one with little access. The only truth was the zero in the checking account, and when there was more than that I slept.

        *   *   *

The Virginia City artist Larry Williamson held an exhibition of his wood and clay sculpture—fanciful, quixotic impressions of birds, fish, horses, and people—inspired from years of artifact gathering in the Great Basin. One wood box sculpture entitled *Geronimo's Cadillac*, incorporated a tin toy car found in a Pioche boneyard. The idea for the sculpture came from a photograph of the Apache warrior in the seat of a 1905 Locomobile. On either side of the shadow box were pictographs of the white man arriving on horseback, a small cross was etched on the saddles. Inside the box were the black eyes and white bone of skulls, up and down the entire back panel of the box. I could not see them until he pointed out the small, nondescript faces. Dozens and dozens of them lost in the brutal exchange of blood for property.

A second sculpture stood on a platform with the iconic title, *How the West Was Won*. The lower two-thirds of the piece was a circular piece of wood, and the top third, again, had small skulls carved in the clay. The entire piece was shaped like an oversized bullet. On its top, a white man galloped on a horse, a pistol in one hand, and a rifle in the other.

Larry taught art for thirty years in southern Nevada. He had many fine artists and poets in his classroom—Tom Gilbertson (who owned the gallery), Gary Short, and others. Jacob Escobedo is an artist who will not forget Larry and Tom's influence. He went on to become a creative force at a major television network. Today Larry lives across the street from the ceramicist Diane Dunn. Another ceramicist, Marta Magistrali, lived around the corner. A master woodworker and artist, Ben and Karen Wesner (my former student who introduced us to Virginia City), live next door to Diane. These artists frame the block that surrounds Community Chest. I try never to lose sight of them, try to remember that art is something that holds us together.

I spent the day at the legislature testifying on the cuts to mental health. How does one win such an argument? The choices rarely change—we will take less and less to do more and more. My colleagues who serve in the august body wished that ours were not testimonies, but imagined stories of people we serve. They are in an untenable position: they would change it if they could, but politics and fear are never far from such discussions, which leaves them wondering how to create a future where our children will thrive, where the story of Nevada becomes an allegory of truth, not fiction. A truth we can embrace, where the needs of our people are held in the same regard as its gold or water.

The artists who live here have a vision of another reality, one that will not wait for legislative approval. To a person these artists live in the margins—they are not showy artists. They create because they must. I take solace in their journeys.

I left the hearings with the paradoxical conclusion that someone listened deeply to the very real consequences of human suffering and yet they are very slow to act upon that information.

Driving home from the legislature, the snow was deep and wild with wind and clouds. All of the ridges were bathed in powder. A huge knuckled universe of white. I tried to think about what I said, that the proposed cuts would harm people, that we needed to do better as a state, that someone should say the dirty word—taxes—that each of us could pound dirt for all that would come of the morning. And yet, the snow on each fertile ridge leading away from here was message enough: we would be all right. The loss of revenue would have deep and irreversible impacts but, with resolve, we would find our way to another snowy day.

CHAPTER SEVEN

Down the Hidden Path to Poetry: Surrender on the Yard

When we returned from Stanford, a friend asked if I would take over his poetry class at the prison (I taught psychology in Western Nevada College's prison program before we left). Naively, I imagined it would be a way to share a subject I love. It was 1989 and I bumbled through my first meeting. The prison is in Carson City, a medium security facility. Something very curious happened: it led me on an odyssey—not unlike founding Community Chest.

One of the first things I did was read poems on specific occasions—to give some definition to the endless cycle of disappearing time. My first winter I read "A Child's Christmas in Wales," imagining Dylan Thomas might assuage something lost inside. I have continued to read this poem every winter. Dylan Thomas was a stranger when I started teaching; he is not a stranger any longer.

I call the gatehouse to ask if the yard is open. The lieutenant tells me to come later, it might be open by two. It is six days before Christmas. I want to read "A Child's Christmas in Wales." I have not missed a year. I do not want to miss this one. By now, only two of the original men are with me. The rest are newbies, some have heard the poem and some have no idea why I would risk bringing up the memory of Christmas, but the atheists have grown to tolerate it. Still I drive down. When I arrive the yard has been opened. This near-winter solstice day will not be in vain.

A new chaplain is in the office. I wave at him to open the chapel. It is a cinderblock room that doubles for a church on the yard. There are two steel doors we must go through. He shakes me off—another disturbance, another program with which to contend. When he gets off his conference call, he opens the doors and apologizes. Twelve men follow me into the barred light of the windows, set up two tables and a dozen chairs. We sit down and I remind them I will read this poem again.

I'm halfway through the poem when a shotgun goes off. What is that, I ask? The guard in the nearby tower is on the loudspeaker: "On your butts, now. Don't move. Sit... down... *now.*" I later find out a fight has broke out in one of the units and the guard called for backup. I cannot hear much more over the din and so I keep reading, determined to finish the poem before we go our separate ways. When it is over, I ask the chaplain to call the gatehouse for our escort. He gets yelled at but he, too, could not hear the recall. We file out in the winter sun. I say goodbye and hope something besides the gun rattle lives on in this day.

*   *   *

I have gone to the prison in all weather but this winter could not have prepared me for what was to come. To be vulnerable on the yard is tantamount to signaling one's failings—you can never let yourself be known—and yet, I ask them to reveal some core of themselves week in and week out, to break that taboo in the service of poetry.

At the last workshop, I asked the men to read the late Ken Brewer's final poems collected in *Whale Song: A Poet's Journey into Cancer.* I had forgotten Darnell already knew too much about this subject.

He is in his early twenties, thin, handsome, from Las Vegas and has no family in northern Nevada. He has come for maybe twenty weeks to write poetry, read voices not known to him. But he has listened carefully and yearned to understand how desert lightning might appear on the page.

When someone like him comes into the workshop I pay attention because he wants more from the written word than escape. He wants to become larger than what he is on the yard. He is willing to go down the hidden path with a room full of strangers from 2:30 until 4:00 until a guard comes to shuffle us back to our respective places. I listen because it is thrilling to open a mind like his.

What I failed to remember was that Darnell is a cancer survivor. When he got the news, he did not know where to turn for help. He had no nearby family to shake him from his worry and had no one on the yard to visit him because he had just arrived at the cattle quarry that is prison. He was sick, sicker than he could have imagined before he understood the slow pummeling of healers, chemotherapy, and darkness. All of it was a ruse for the cell that makes its own rules and heeded nothing he told it until Darnell could hardly speak. His mother sent notes asking for his forgiveness: the bills, the kids, her own bedraggled health, and the worn-out car conspired against visiting him. This left him to blister in the infirmary from the overwork of muscles tending to their survival.

I have resolved that to teach in prison you must forget the rules, the ordinary prescriptions for inquiry, in fact, you mostly forget that it is teaching at all. I think of it as closer to meeting friends for a serious conversation, for food or water in a landscape that regards food and water as contraband. It's not that the metaphor of food is particularly applicable; rather, it is that they partake of poetry as if it were sustenance, as if it equipped them for speaking of more than their lives inside.

With forgetting I blunder. Not even for a minute did I understand how far Darnell would drift until he patiently asked to share his response to Ken's last poems, entitled "A Whale's Song." At times, when he read it, there was such overwhelming silence you could hear us gasp, you could infer something grave was conferred upon the listener. Darnell took us in his hands and urged us to follow, coupled his whale song with the defiant killing of cancer. He never let up until the sounding of whales from depths, the moan that sonar might record, whispered back to the surface to complete his journey.

A quiet storm
Rain drops full of demise
Devouring, eating away at my existence like acid rain
The pain
When I look in the mirror I see a monster
An undesirable creature
A sick, frail, disgusting shell made of raw sewage
Something a vulture or maggot wouldn't eat
Useless
Something so vile,
it'll make God's eyes burn looking at such a thing
With Cancer's shadow never leaving my side
day and night
My soul weeps

My soul sings a whale's song
Hmm mmM
Hmm mmM
Hmm mmM
    Mmm…

This, I imagine, is what Ken Brewer had hoped for: to scramble the alphabet of cancer and save one person from its sentence. To think that it happened in a room where the word *sentence* has such a malevolent connotation is a miracle of flight, a possible redemption in the chapel of our meeting. Not one person spoke for a full minute. Finally, interminably, I offered: "You have just written your breakthrough poem." Johnny looked across the room and announced, "When I am sixty, I will remember the day you read your first poem. By then you will be in books and people will know your name is Darnell." We waited in that odd pause of kindness and hesitation, not knowing what to do. It sounded like a whale had sung from the abyssal zone, and then it reverberated into the percussive silence of the yard.

This has happened a handful of times in the workshop. Cliff wrote his breakthrough poem and curiously, it was a whale song too. I had challenged the men to respond to Pablo Neruda's question: why was there no literature about the narwhal? Well, cocky, quick-wit Cliff hunkered down to write his answer, which he would read when I returned in the fall (I teach from September to June). Again, the sounding of a species rose from the sea floor and we shook in recognition: your poem is like the most wild of Borges's beasts. "Requiem Narwhal" begins where we can only imagine such beings exist:

> Hard surface blow, held breath
> and the final
> spiral
> descent
> begins on bars of sifting sunlight….

Cliff held the poem close until he set the paper down. It was as if it had confirmed his willingness to be known, to be revealed to the others. That is the gift of the workshop: the poem is a messenger through which the participants can distinguish their identity, their transitory presence—even when it is for a decade or two. They can become something greater than the flesh that anchors them to chow at 7, and 11, and 4, to the thrice-daily count that refutes one's absence, or the simplicity of release. It is, after all, an angel that presides over the workshop. There are very few reasons for its continuing life: outside the chapel, the yard is filled with pigeons and seagulls and the doors swing but one way. The irony of admission is that prison infers completion, and yet there are men floating in the arms of parole decisions that will never be completed. To resurrect a sense of self in this environment, let alone a poem, to think you are audacious enough to read a poem in this place, requires the razor, the knife, the ordinary tools of intimidation be laid to rest. The tuition, while steep and unforgiving, is a vow that is taken without my knowledge. They insist on taking it, each in their own way, to affirm admission in the small gathering of minds on Tuesdays in the chapel. In this we share our belief in each other, and in poetry. We belong to a ritual of reading, study, and writing—but finally, what is taken from this time is a subtle assurance that with each other, we will be all right.

Outside the chapel, there are morning glories, hollyhocks, and cosmos. It is one of the few places there is color on the yard. The other is at the turn to the gatehouse. A garden of meticulously cared for flax, phlox, and cosmos decorate a monument to Vietnam vets. Some days the men water the grass at its borders for hours. I have often wished such flowers grew in my yard, often wanted them to bear color in the rust of our soil. But I do not put forth the effort. I am not left alone with time.

To be fair, there are the occasional hands that reach in from beyond the fence to intercede with the gift of books: six volumes on Japanese, Sumi-e, word origins, a dictionary of symbols, and a thin volume of tattooed gothic girls. Maybe these books will help me teach Johnny who paints and writes things that poets yearn to do in their forties—which he is. Now, however, after years in the workshop, he can tell Darnell why his poem was not just good, but original, and why the constant refrain of moans from endless sea water was onomatopoeic, and why the internal rhythm was likened to the cells which would be defeated, and why the reader would be swept into its consciousness, and why, without intending, it elevated our experience to that transcendent place we reserve for Tuesdays, and why, most of all, he would never look back to write something smaller. In short, Johnny told him why he had just freed the written word from its cage.

This was not always the case. When Johnny first came into the workshop Stan cut him off fast: "You can't write this shit—what is this stuff?" Johnny listened to Stan—freckled, red headed, smoked Camels—and tried to live within the bounds of the workshop. Stan and he became very close and Johnny became a poet.

Johnny is a short Mexican with a moustache. He grew up in the California desert. His family drives ten hours to sit with him in visiting, fidgeting with candy. When we held the art show at the Sun Mountain Artworks in Virginia City, they came. Even though he was not there, they needed to be with his art. He has worked on a book since starting in the workshop. "I try to write like Jimmy Baca."

"Write like yourself." He is tired of hearing this from me and hands me another poem about women, having grown up in a family of women:

…Unless I conjure
the quiet earth of my heart,
I cannot sustain your breath
laced in my hair as we broke
the eucharist of our bodies,
then drew down
the moon's white gaze
to wash the parchment
of blood and seed
into the cool koi pond.

I think Johnny will survive but I cannot promise him he will be released.

Ray started to speak. Ray is reticent, been down over two decades. Words like *down* take on new meaning in prison: under, lower, beneath others, below time. Words do not come easy for the Vietnam vet. He has aged and is getting smaller. Sometimes he nods off in class. I don't know if he will get out.

He would rather listen than offer his insight to a poem, a trait all of us find immensely calming. Ray knew there was little more to be said about Darnell's poem until this: "This poem will change you. You will not see this art in the same way. You will need it now, like we need it." Ray spoke like he wrote his poems: epigrammatic and vulnerable. That V-word again: what was required to partake of the workshop. Ray is a chaplain's assistant and he studies the Bible like his poetry, culling from the text small bits of insight.

Then Darnell did something even more surprising. Now that he was in remission, the prison was anxious to return him closer to his Las Vegas home. They needed the beds, an irony that was not lost on us: a thousand men had been cramped into a facility for half that number for years. Darnell asked if he could stay—in the workshop, that is, asked if he could participate for the duration, asked if he could *join*. I stammered, knowing family is also like food or water in this place, and without it, one veers to the ends of feeling, becomes part of the cycle that is prison. He repeated the words: *"I want to stay."*

I called the prison staff the next day to ask if they could make an exception, if they would permit him to study poetry with the others. I sounded foolish, trying to make his request sound important, rationalizing the journey he had begun, trying to make words to describe the poem buried in the depths of a whale's song, trying to find some explanation for his survival. This is often where it ends, where art stumbles into the dust on the yard, and the wish is exonerated in the flight of sparrows or the men who walk just feet beyond the fence to pronounce f-r-e-e-d-o-m in slow, penitent stares, the short-timers who no longer have to ask for permission to study such a trivial thing as poetry. I hung up the phone knowing I was not like the brilliant public defender I would soon meet who had dedicated her life to saying what peace might come from mercy. I could only hope now that some part of those words would be understood. Emigrants in our own language, that's what we were.

After Darnell read his poem, Joe read his love songs, Johnny charted his gothic girls through another romp, and I muttered some indifferent praise: Johnny, too, had just triumphed and sent one over the transom that would be published, and Preston came from the edge of the table to read a poem twisted to such ends I could not understand it.

Not long ago I gave a poetry reading from a book of bird poems that took me seven years to write, *Woodsmoke, Wind, and the Peregrine*, an initiation that meant little on the *inside*. When I finished someone asked what it was that kept me in the workshop. I could not answer and shuffled through the obvious reasons, but ultimately it is faith that propels me to art in the face of all deterrents. I continued until I remembered the men's faces and knew it was nothing more than the rising of hope where none should dare to hope and that in so doing, we found a reason to return to the poem that let us indulge this small desire.

Just as this routine becomes expected, the odyssey turns us from the room. Hope plays tricks on us and the gate closes for good like it did on Tillman after he read *his* breakthrough poem. Tillman wanted desperately to belong to the workshop. After weeks and weeks of trying he read "The Last Poem." Three days later he staged his suicide by kidnapping the prison doctor: he knew the guards would shoot him and they did. He was in prison for killing a cop and after repeated denials by the parole board, he chose to leave us with violence. I could not resolve his actions, could only return with my books to begin the workshop again. The men came knowing Tillman had left, had gone into the dust of that hot afternoon. Tillman took something from our time together, nothing so grand as innocence, but his death was a reminder to pay attention. None of us read between the lines of his prescient poem to see what he would do.

Left in the crosshairs of death and poetry, I knew even less of what to teach, what to believe of the line from Milosz: "What is poetry that does not save/ Nations or people?"

CHAPTER EIGHT

Making Do

I was upstairs at my desk at Community Chest and noticed a thin line crawling down the wall, over the painting and onto the books. It was a few years after we bought the building in 1995. I followed it up the roofline to a hole with light. The upstairs roof had 2 X 1 slats on the cross members—about two inches apart. The shingles covered the gap. There was no insulation and no plywood sheathing. All met on the steep ridge over my head. I continued to stare until I realized the shingles had finally given in to the fifty-mile-an-hour winds on the Divide. It was not uncommon to feel the third story move while sitting at my desk. I just hoped it stayed on most of the foundation— there were cement stem walls under two-thirds of the building. My neighbor's house moved one foot off the bricks in a bad windstorm. The entire length of our building faced south to the Carson Valley, so it was like a sail in those winds. The tongue-and-groove siding needed paint every three years, and I had hoped the roof would last another ten—until we could pay the building off. I made a deal: if the roofers would take payments of $1,000 a month for the balance, I would put a metal roof on. Thirty-two thousand dollars later we said yes.

Grants and contracts have multiple line items from which to draw expenses—roofing is not one of them. This had to come from another source. As did all of the repairs. The downstairs doors—the lower tiers of the south-facing sail—looked worse than the hull of a wooden boat. In the winter the wind blew the snow and the rain under the sill until they swelled to affirm their disgust, which was fine unless you needed to use them. The doors were replaced when we bought the building and still the requests came: "More varnish, that will save them… more WD-40 on the lock and please, please, can you fix the latch that seems to have fallen from the door jam." These conversations are logged in the notebook of subtle pleasures—and I record the latest entry with ease: the toilet has swallowed its third gallon and it will not stop; the copier is speaking in tongues; the food pantry has an overgrown onion in it and the donors cannot understand how it got there; someone has taken the emergency pager from the wall and the man outside is very upset at his wife; the computer will not find its perfect mate on the Internet highway and so you remain lost in the ether; the grant is due but no one seems to know why it needs a staple rather than a paper clip, and your good friend calls to tell you it has been denied because a new staff member chose wrong; you have to make six copies of the audit to request a budget amendment—when they all say the same thing: you do not lie, cheat, or steal; the car has bald tires but the spare is new; there is a mouse in the toaster but thank God it is only a small one; the student who thinks of himself as Houdini is hanging from a seat belt in the back of the van, but the unflappable driver cuts him loose just as he is about to stop breathing; the waves keep coming in without a young swimmer until finally one of the group reaches him in the riptide.

Every executive director could go on with the notebook for days. It is a requirement of the job to laugh at oneself because most of the carnival is just that, except mistakes are for keeps: for almost nine months I knew something was wrong—money I put aside was depleted, receipts did not equal deposits, and checks arrived intermittently. I went over the books more and more often and still the revenue was not accounted for. I asked and asked the accountant for statements, balances, withdrawals, and there was a polite smile, deferent and willing to please. But it was not an answering smile. When I finally fired the accountant she had embezzled more than $15,000.

In court, I testified that several thousand dollars in cash had also been stolen but I could not prove it. The feckless lawyer and the alcoholic DA were implacable—nearly thieves themselves—and so my remarks became the very tools the defendant's counsel used against me. Somehow, in the twilight of legal repose the defendant received probation with restitution to follow. Two checks later she was on the lamb. I tried calling parole and probation for several years and finally decided it was cheap tuition: never lose sight of your money.

The real thrills were yet to come: after the defendant embezzled ten times our loss from a California business, her parole officer called to tell me that I would never see the money because the lawyers for the most recent theft were first in line. And she had to do ten years before parole was considered.

Years later, Debby and I stayed in Ely at the Nevada Hotel—a throwback to the 30s with Hollywood black and whites in each room, a stuffed animal parade in the casino, a perfectly restored Indian scooter under glass, and a boa skin the entire length of the dining area. Debby came upstairs to tell me there was someone in the coffee shop but hinted there was more. When I sat down, this person came to the table and sat next to me, nervous, awkward, and said, "You may never forgive me but I am sorry. I will repay all of it before I die."

This is part of the notebook too: the hand that unfolds to forgive. For a while I did receive checks and then not much more. But they were off the drugs and living in relative peace. It has happened to many friends who run businesses, and each of us know the desperation of greed and grief.

*   *   *

With the new building we were able to start many programs because we had space. The thrift store and food closet operated out of the downstairs. A public health nurse worked in a cramped closet adjacent to the furnace. We bought a used bus from the Sheriff's office for a dollar and Cindy Boyd started the Classroom on Wheels, a mobile early childhood education program. She was the Pied Piper with preschoolers. I have never met a woman who derived so much joy driving a bus and teaching children. She could do both things with aplomb. Her enthusiasm was contagious. She knew exactly how to get the attention of her little tribe and they listened intently as she read to them, taught them to use a pencil, scissors, and clay. She helped them onto the swings, the ladders, and the slide in the park by her bus. She was the most demonstrative early childhood educator I knew. In Cindy, we saw the future of early childhood education: there could be buses in every community. And she could lead that project.

We hired Paula Scott to expand the before- and after-school program for elementary youth to thirty youth per day. In the summer more than fifty youth participated. We hired staff before we had desk space because the needs were constant and pressing. We offered domestic violence counseling, substance abuse and family counseling. We began working with counseling interns. It was dizzying; we did not know what all of this really involved. Meanwhile I continued my work on the homeless education program.

One of the VISTA Volunteers with whom we began, Shannon Montana, was adamant we operate the food closet and thrift store on a barter basis. She insisted on this because of her own experience: taking food or clothing is embarrassing. If you give something in return your dignity remains intact. She had watched many members of her family struggle for years despite their hard work and best intentions. Shannon helped us to understand that people living in poverty are not lazy; rather, they feel trapped by their circumstances. She was right-- what did I know of taking food for hunger? The food closet became the gatehouse for our many services, the place through which the families could access other supports. Shannon treated these families with respect, which gave them hope that they could receive similar respect in our programs. This was a groundbreaking shift in how we did business: not for, but with those we served.

Similarly, Paula Scott, our before- and after-school program coordinator, knew about raising kids right. She had struggled with being beautiful but not taken seriously and was determined that the children she taught would have both self-respect and value learning. Reading and writing became her crucible. She never wanted the kids to experience a learning environment without love and academic support. The kids flocked to her and she developed a reputation for teaching that was unparalleled.

Debby and I mentored these young people who came to Community Chest to learn something of themselves and others. We had no idea this initial core group would become the backbone of our beliefs and values. Because of their input, their influence on our work, Debby and our team drafted our guiding principles at our first annual retreat, which guide us to this day:

> We are brought together to do very important work that cannot be accomplished alone. It is not a coincidence that we are here today, although we may move on to other places and organizations in the future.

> Our work is as much about our own spiritual growth and that of this planet's as it is about addressing needs and strengths of children, families, and people in our community.

> We all have ideas, talents, special qualities that need to be honored and encouraged to make our work together more successful. We each take responsibility for creating a role that is meaningful and that fits with our talents as well as supports the overall mission of the organization.

> We are part of this organization by choice and with that realization, we will direct our energy to the growth and health of the organization as well as to the work we accomplish through the organization, until that point we are ready to move on.

> We are a transforming organization and accept that we are involved in carving out new and sometimes ambiguous ways of doing our lifework.

> We will support each other taking risks, making decisions, making mistakes, and achieving our goals.

> We will listen carefully to each other to learn what our next steps must be to fulfill our vision. We are willing to look as critically at ourselves as at each other, and to recognize and accept that we may have some shortcomings and barriers that need to be overcome if we are to bring the best we have to offer to the

organization. The group agrees to support one another in this effort, to be honest and direct our concerns to the individual team members in a respectful and caring manner.

We are envisioning an effort that we will remain committed to despite current funding or resources. That is, we'll pursue whatever we need to make this happen. Our vision is doable and there are resources to support the vision.

We will utilize all ideas to work to our advantage—giving credit and building on our collective strength.

We believe the philosophy and the process are as much of what we're about as the programs we support.

We are creating a new model for doing business; we will not replicate what we know doesn't work or that places someone or some agency below and some above. We support shared leadership and decision-making toward a shared goal.

*   *   *

Late in the 1990s a young man joined us from Oregon. Two years out of graduate school he had met and married a woman from Reno. When he arrived he had a bushy ponytail and was filled with idealism. Debby and I thought we had found a leader in Erik Schoen, someone with whom we could confide and trust to grow the business. He is fond of retelling this story: he interviewed by designing an activity with Paula's youth. If he couldn't work with kids, it wasn't the job for him. He had them eating out of his hands. We offered him the position and wrote down a list of things to begin. He went home to Oregon, packed up his things and arrived to work. The last line on his list: "Enjoy your first weeks at Community Chest. Debby and I are on vacation." In retrospect this seemed slightly egregious to be gone when our new employee showed up for work but it proved to be the one thing we did right: give people the latitude to create their own positions, to develop their passions and put them into practice. This was worth more than any amount of money we could give them. It meant people had to work with autonomy. This did not work for everyone but for those it did, they became dedicated, fierce in their commitment to Community Chest and to building the non-profit that Debby so eloquently aspired to in our guiding principles. Paula, Shannon, Erik, and Cindy were the stalwarts that grew the organization. They stayed with us while we worked for statewide change on homeless education and service-learning. They let us go about our work while they built the house that became Community Chest.

Equally important, they helped us to endure the storms. The vile missives that were in the newspaper, that arrived via certified mail from our detractors, were intolerable. At night Debby and I asked each other if we should quit. They threatened her with everything but physical violence. Our lawyer, the husband of Emma Sepúlveda, the Chilean poet I translated, John Mulligan, wrote letter after letter to them but they would not desist. Some of the commissioners and, I suspect, many in the community thought we were unfit for this work because of this spurious influence. At one point we were called a vile epitaph not worthy of response, save it was our livelihood. Hatred by any other name is toxic. I worried constantly about the effect it was having on our children: would they suffer at school, would they hear the taunts in the halls? It tested us, forced Debby and me and our small team to question what we believed, if we believed. I thought I was strong but I did not know what strength was required to endure constant public humiliation.

CHAPTER NINE

Mountains Above Manzanar

Mountains above Manzanar, that's where I imagined Jess to be, not outside the barbed compound where his parents had been relocated. Jess's parents did not know each other when they arrived at Manzanar as children. They might have played in the dust of Lone Pine, imagined Mt. Whitney to be Mt. Fuji, thought of soy and fish, the market his grandfather ran, the spinet her mother had in the living room, the letters to the island of paper cranes. One winter which grew into every winter in our late twenties, on our way to ski at Mammoth, Jess and I stopped in the pre-dawn light: I imagined them eating from rice bowls under guard towers, asking for news of the fight, trying to guess which way was the road home, what man to believe on the radio, and then I thought, did they ever believe anything? How did they feel that first winter morning that became four winters until the ghostly clouds rose over Nagasaki?

I listened, a rag doll with no voice, could not explain my lapse in history, my determination to apologize. The war, I wanted to say, was not ours, but I could not believe my words. Jess knew his history like a checkerboard. His parents had recited the loss of livelihood, residence, and dignity to him and his sister so often it became a hymn of family sorrow.

They were not alone. Years later, when his mother was interviewed for an oral history on Manzanar, hers became part of the flood of recollections at this camp: yes, that was true, but there was more she could not confide to a tape recorder. Neither she nor his father dwelled on it. Rather, they tried to compensate for the hollow period of years by work, effort at redemption, and reading to their children. They schooled them in this country's mores so that as they aged, this tongue, this intolerant vengeance would never speak again.

"What island did they live on," he asked, "the island they came from, or the island here in the States?" They could not afford the luxury of choice. His father worked harder and harder to get as much education as possible so that in time, his master's degree permitted a mastery of engineering. His mother gave Jess and his sister enough love to understand why his work was needed.

As we stood there on that morning Jess wanted that island to disappear, wanted the monument to slide into the ground, the lone guard tower to fall on its beams. Jess wanted Manzanar to skulk from view on the desert floor. It was only now, in this light, that he could see it as something other than a cage for his parents. This pre-dawn light was a portent of the mountains rising above Manzanar in which he sealed their sorrow on that isolated plot at the base of the eastern Sierra.

We drove to Bishop in silence, ate breakfast and began to feel some movement in our limbs. The day was bright—winter had come at last and we were almost on skis.

Perhaps it was this imagined place, mountains above Manzanar, that Jess stared into on that ridge when we took our first group hiking, or years later when we pushed our bikes into Hobart Lake. Perhaps there was a topo map that connected something far from any earth and its contours and led to a valley of forgiveness. In my twenties I didn't believe there was such a place. In my fifties, it was so real that he could be buried there. Jess took us on a long journey. Most of the time we were lost. Despite his protestations, I followed, foolishly thinking my friendship was solace for what he could not share. It was all I could *do*—listen to the man who drove the Ford Econoline van out of Bishop.

*　　　　　*　　　　　*

After more than ten years with the school, Jess called it quits. He moved to South Lake Tahoe and took a job as a special education coordinator to stop the hemorrhage of debt. I was thrilled he lived closer—one hour from Virginia City—and worked for Karen Wesner's brother-in-law, Rich Fischer. Jess moved in with him and soon the basement looked like the trailer—except it was in one room. For once I could see him without a four-hour drive to Redding. For once, we could be together to push our bikes into Hobart, to share meals, to have him in the life of our sons.

Jess sat at our kitchen table in Virginia City. His respect for Debby only strengthened his promise to teach Nevada everything: how to fish, hunt Bambi (although she and I loathed guns), and ski. Maybe, he offered, he'd read and hike with him. Jess became the constant voice of concern, returning to our lives when they spun out of control. When he held Nevada it was with the pride of a parent, a logical extension of his flesh "by association." If he couldn't have a son in this moment, he could share ours. Love was not kind to him and Nevada was his surrogate son.

Later that spring Jess called to say Joe was in the hospital. "What?" I said, incredulous that a logger could be anywhere near medical care.

"Could you visit him when you get a chance?"

"How long's he been in there?" but it didn't matter. Joe's wife said it was serious and Jess couldn't get away to see him. I told him I'd find a way but wished that I was going for some other reason. Joe was a stalwart friend to Jess and I hated to see him fall. But he was in a good hospital and if any man could get better, it was Joe. Still, he and his wife were alone in that Bay Area hospital, a long way from Redding, from their kids, and nothing I could do would change that. Somehow this signaled that things had begun to change. We were no longer exempt from the phone call that separated us from those we loved. Soon I would be reporting to Jess on our mutual friend. Soon I would become the person he relied on for information about the inside of the hospital room, about the quality of care, about the way in which Joe was looking out the window.

*   *   *

"Meet me on the West Shore at 5:30 and we'll get out by sunrise." Naturally, being at Lake Tahoe, Jess had to find out how to catch Mackinaw—Tahoe's deep-water trout.

"The West Shore?" I asked, as if Joe's old boat would make it across a duck pond. The boat was Joe's going away gift to Jess. I stood on the dock at Camp Richardson. It was about 5:00 A.M. I knew he'd sleep right through and leave me standing there till dawn, too late to get the boat in the water and fish. It was cold, starlit, not a sound. I couldn't see one navigation light on the lake. Then, almost imperceptibly, I heard a motor from the north. It was a few minutes after 5:30, still black and I couldn't make out a vessel. The bow light was nearly at the dock when Jess called out, "Get in."

"I didn't think you'd make it in the wind. How'd you get here?"

"I came over last night."

"It was blowing 25-30 miles per hour at the house."

"I put in at Cave Rock at 8:00. Three hours later I dropped anchor at Baldwin Beach."

"You drove into the waves for three hours in this boat with those same crappy Evinrudes?"

"It was slow going."

Taciturn to a fault. "Get in, we're wasting time." Not a hint of worry. He thought the downriggers—eight-pound lead weights on steel line with a leader— should be at 200 feet. He idled over the shelf until a small image appeared on the fish finder. "Drop it," and I let the downrigger fly.

Fishing for Mackinaw is unlike any fishing I have done. It's hard to feel the fish bite because the hook is so far below. The only way to verify a strike is to reel in the line but the Mackinaw dies on the way up—the gills are not equipped for the lack of oxygen in shallow water. By mid-morning we had a few strikes and one small Mackinaw. I called it the two-hundred-dollar fish. The equipment costs more than buying a Mackinaw from a charter boat.

"How's Joe," he asked? I had seen Joe the past week.

"Not very well. The tumor's the size of a grapefruit. They've got him in a room facing the redwoods. The nurses thought it would make him feel better."

When I visited Joe his wife was in the room. Their kid's pictures were taped to the window. He was trying to laugh in that garrulous way of his, trying to dodge the stone in his throat. "I'll be fine. Ain't no goddamn cancer gonna put me down."

"Sure," I said, half-believing the truth of his desire. "When will they know if the marrow takes?"

"Not for a few weeks."

"But this is experimental, right?"

"It's my only shot. If I wasn't a logger this would have been over by now."

Joe's wife looked at me to confide: it's still not over. The cancer room is always filled with hope. There is little that can penetrate its resistance. It is its own true north. The patient, Joe, his wife, and their children at home in Redding live by the habitual routine of waking to monitors, injections, feedings, nausea, the burn of chemo, the opiates, and the occasional news from the oncologist. "In two weeks you can expect function to return, but it may take longer. In rare cases, we have seen memory deficits that linger for months, even years. I would not plan on returning to the chainsaw for a living." And then, almost as quickly, the news is over. The questions begin. She looked at Joe and tried to ask, "Who will support…" but could not finish and held him for minutes.

The cancer room is small, the patient dependent on the reports from the outside world. Joe sails on a sea of medical interruptions, his arms blue from the widening tubes taped to his wrist. When we leave his face turns from us as if to say *I will be here when you return*. The cancer room calls him by his diagnosis. He answers without thought: I'm going home. Going to what I know—my job, my wife, my sixteen-year-old who wants to me to hunt with him this weekend. And still, the echo of conversation in the hall: he may not pull through. In the cancer room, you learn not to listen, learn to keep the antenna down, to mask the disappointment with resolve. Grief sets up camp in the corner of the room. It is an unseen shrine, always present. There are candles, a rosary of God, tiny flowers that someone placed in a cup, the faint smell of cinnamon or is it the scent of roses from the candle-lit vision, the eyes almost drawn to a close? Joe tells me he sees things in the corner, imagines someone standing there trying to argue with the bad cells, but sometimes they lose. They leave the room with their head down. They cannot speak up or disagree. They say the argument is over. Joe says someone comes back to ask if it is really over but then he drifts until the nurse wakes him. The morphine has many tongues and he asks them for permission to go home where he knows what to say but each day is a climb from the bed to the toilet, something he has not rehearsed. When we leave the routine starts over, the next shift, the next day begins without hesitation.

CHAPTER TEN

The Board of Pardons Hearing

Carson City: I have just come from Northern Nevada Correctional Center to Nevada's Supreme Court. If the act of writing poetry comes at any risk, it is the risk of dissent, but what can that mean to a poet in prison? It can only mean that you write to stay alive. Inside, the trappings of art trap nothing; in fact, they release the men to imagine what it is like to have a voice in the choir.

This is what I found myself thinking when Ray stood before the Board of Pardons to ask for mercy: seven state Supreme Court justices, the attorney general, and the governor. All morning the public defender, a wisp of a woman, pled for their understanding, their judicial courage in the face of victims, district attorneys, and the persistent drum of public safety. There were free men and women who walked through the same metal detector as me to ask for their voting rights, their gun rights, their driving rights, or their parental rights to be restored. Over and over, they shook like Lilliputians before the dais. Their families sat in the rows beside me, all of them severed from the threads of normal employment, housing, and movement because a loved one had made a mistake. In some cases a horrible mistake.

This is where the judges started to listen and question, sitting above us with case files and recommendations, histories of the wronged and wrongdoing, the confluence of the helpless before the imminence of justice. The governor sat in the middle of the group and led the discussions. More than once, members of the board confided: "I do not look forward to this day," a day they are compelled to participate in twice a year. More than 280 requests are made for the two dozen cases that will be heard—each of them balanced before the court like a knife. "It is shameful," the chief justice admonished, "that we cannot adjudicate the hundreds of requests because of time alone."

One week before the hearing, the public defender called me at the house. It was 8 P.M. I could not believe she was at the office, preparing her cases for the coming Wednesday. "Tell me about the poems Ray wrote. Send me the ten poems that underscore his remorse, his understanding of the life he took." She talked for more than twenty minutes, wanting to know every detail about him, about his desire to return to the outside, his participation in the workshop. I hung up the phone, incredulous that someone like her could be working on his behalf, unknown to him, unknown to me, trying in the unforgiving light of the penal system to find forgiveness.

For the next three days I read Ray's poems to find the precise language that would exonerate him before the court. What can art possibly mean in this context? What a foolish question. It would perform a function, it would have a very real utility: to save a life. I didn't have to read far: Ray understood long before I arrived that he had stepped way beyond any semblance of acceptable human behavior. He had taken his beloved's life, and it was killing him now much as he killed her then. One of the poems I shared with the public defender closes with the line: "the slow, lethal injection of time without parole." A judge did not have to be a poet to understand its significance.

The next day she called me back. She wanted more information. She needed to know like Plato needed to know the verity of his remorse. Again, we reviewed the poems. Again, she asked for clarification: did this one *really* mean he asked for forgiveness? Did he understand the severity of his crime? Did he believe in his minimalist lines that he was responsible for this heinous act?

Like Darnell's question, "Can I stay in the workshop," I stammered, afraid to answer her because I believed Ray had known remorse to be a shadow that would not leave him. I could not promise the poems would infer this, I could not tell her they were the ones that would free him. It was only then that the stakes became apparent—this was something far greater than poetry: it was a life-saving attempt to show that his fragmented world had somehow come together to represent a unified whole. He would speak through these ten sinewy poems, his peace. They would act on his behalf, like emissaries to another country, the country of disbelief.

When I faxed a few more poems, she called again to review them for their separate meanings, their isolated truths, weighing one against the other like grains of sand. There was no literary sanctuary here. He had to live with the consequence of his words. They had to find a purchase, a place of equality in the cheapened marketplace of language and the ever-present past that rarely exonerates its survivors. Slowly I read "My Living Room" into the phone:

> My living room has a
> Window that tries to feed
> The ebb and flow of
> Dark cold musty indifferent yet
> Like the tombs of Pharaoh's still
> My living room has a door—
> Its silence sings me back
> From life's lock-down death.

By the time she stood to begin her defense of Ray, we had heard at least six people whose lives would cascade in the balance of a vote—some to be granted clemency, some to be returned to their shadows. The governor asked to be recused from voting on the prior case: the victim was one of his best friends. In a complicated system designed to ensure that the decision to grant mercy was considered by all nine members of the board, the governor had to cast a vote. The chief justice patiently reminded him of this fact. For more than a minute he held his face in his hands and finally, almost inaudibly, said "OK, I can do it." Then he, too, voted in the affirmative, citing his friend's desire to do the right thing, saying he would not want revenge. A more humane consequence of violence I have not witnessed.

Was it the consequence of art that drew its breath once again? We were reading *Hope Against Hope* by Osip Mandelstam's wife, Nadezhda, in the workshop. Chapter by chapter, Ray had asked for more of the unforgiving tale, the time when Stalin made literature into a landscape of fear, when the young poets visited Osip seeking counsel, only to give him up for their silly tongues. And because we had been through the lives and work of Lorca, Machado, Hernández and the others whom the fascists could not countenance, her story resonated with the longer narrative of living with terror and writing poetry anyway. Ray never presumed to have stature as an artist, he did not want to be freed because his work was of merit. He wanted to be heard for what he was: a man in search of his life, a man who was by now in his fifties, wearing frayed shirts and a Vietnam vet baseball cap, a man who wrote poems to his family for the birthdays and the holidays missed. He was a lay chaplain and spent weeks on end trying to find resolution in that room. I had become close to the prison chaplains with whom he worked, each of them drawn like birds to the concertina wire. I cannot say what brings a religious man to prison, but they come and they keep coming as if to drown out the fear that shackles atheists and believers alike. They try not to judge, try only to offer solace. Which is what we were coming to that morning.

Again I floated back to Ray and the public defender. She began timorously, then found her ground, having done this for eighteen years, having rehearsed how it would be with each member of the august body, having reminded them that this was a board of mercy. After reviewing the details of his case, she did something quite unexpected: she chose three poems to demonstrate his grave sorrow, his refuge in the expression of contrition. There were no masks to cover him from the suggestion of grief, from the inference of living with his guilt. He stood beside her, solemn, quivering like the others before him, listening as her remarks echoed across the bench. At the end of the proceedings, Ray asked to speak. After a few words, he began to slowly chant a poem, holding the words in midair until his breath caught, and he continued to release them in this most unlikely of rooms. The board watched as he pushed on through the final stanza to measure out whatever justice would come from this: he had spoken. The prison staff recommended an immediate and full commutation of his sentence given his age and good behavior, and the Board of Pardons followed suit. None of us were prepared for this act of kindness. But I am loath to be prepared for anything in prison except that we can return to art.

I hugged the public defender, this small person I did not know just weeks before, this public servant who had literally saved Ray's life, hugged Ray's girlfriend, and drove home, not believing what I had heard and seen in all the morning's cases. Lives bent to grass, and some, resurrected from that same grass like Whitman writ large but without notice. I tried to share what had happened with my family and of course, could only babble snippets. It was like having been to a private screening of Beckett and trying to summarize it. All I could remember was the playwright's mantra: "Art is not a mirror held up to reality but a hammer with which to shape it."

Three months later, the parole board—all of whom serve at the pleasure of the governor—rejected Ray's request and returned him to the state's custody for another three years. They did so in direct opposition to the decision by the Board of Pardons. He is still in prison after being denied parole yet again.

*　　　　　*　　　　　*

Adrienne Rich said that writing a poem is an act of revolution; it is a political act. Many American poets have echoed her sentiment, but how does that affect the men in the workshop where I'm repeatedly asked to define what makes a good poem? I defer to the obvious rhythms and routines but they rarely satisfy and so have had to cobble together a penal guide of poetic reference. Penal because it doesn't matter what goes on outside—they must write despite the ebb and flow of culture and literary taste—and poetic because they persist as poets. By now, Johnny and Ray and the others can recite what it is that brings such sweet satisfaction to our meeting. But none of us could articulate what happened in that courtroom. None of us could articulate what Ray's poem said in defense of its author.

When I run out of resources, I surrender, having little to hide my ignorance of our mutual desire to know. Reading from another book of essays, I found myself returning to Wordsworth and shortly after that, Edwin Muir—poets who could not forsake the grit of daily life. This is all too simplified but in prison words come and go like the high desert wind from the valley floor—which is where it *is*—and there is usually nothing to defend against them. And so we are made vulnerable again. It's practical, this knowledge we accumulate, but that may be what we need.

What teaches most is not the answer, but the struggle. I share the struggle to understand the skill of these poets every time we meet.

My name for this process is the journey to anonymity in art. The journey to the absence of ego in the face of those things that cannot be distinguished but are nevertheless known. In other words, I teach as if we are compelled to turn to poetry for wisdom or the shadowy truth, the verification of our very selves, not as separate from, but joined with a common knowledge, even if it is in my case, and therefore the men in the workshop, the recognition of how little we may ever know. We journey together as aspirants in a granular reality—whether thief or teacher—alone in our separate existences, yet singular in purpose: to write from this experience, a poem.

I am constantly asked by the men to reconcile the void between their experience inside and what they read in the contemporary poem, which may have something to do with their code of poetic labor: the bullshit factor. They don't care who is right or wrong. They want to read and write without the mind jesting. They already know the obvious: no amount of this jesting will lead them to confront the day any wiser. "You have a responsibility," I begin, "to the others in the room." In the chapel that audience is a dozen men, the place of their reckoning.

Seamus Heaney wrote "The end of art is peace," the same Heaney whose translation of *Beowulf* we read and reread for the nuanced sounds of Gaelic and Old English, and whose early poems we read to hear the cadences of craft. There's no wool to be pulled over the men's eyes; they are open to the possibilities of poetry, not imitated art as Wordsworth reminds them, but the effect of being fully exposed to the chaos and order of their lives.

*   *   *

The men in the workshop write and edit a literary journal, *Razor Wire*. A curious thing happened: after a half-dozen annual issues, poets from the outside wrote to ask if their work might be included. I deferred to the men: it was their journal, they had to choose. They finally relented but only so long as they could have the final say on its contents. Something else happened: the small black journal began to acquire status. People wanted to be in it, read from it, contribute art to it, and have their books reviewed in it. This has always been a paradox to us: why would someone want to see his or her work in a prison journal? But I think the reason is clear: there is no pretense in the journal. There is the idea that art could spare a life. When you write in the face of a life sentence, you cannot afford the indignity of posing. They shoot one another down at the first hint of any such behavior. They are resigned to winnowing poetry from their lives—real and imagined—and the measure of their art will be the depth of the life from which it springs—as Joyce has said.

I do not hold the men in the workshop up as a paragon or an example. They fight, they argue, and they cry. They return like the days on the calendar, in the unforgiving and persistent rattle of time, to create an echo of resistance, that may, in its flight, become the heralded poem so long anticipated by Darnell or Ray or Johnny or Preston. They have been the recipients of literary fellowships, interviewed and exploited by some in the national media, published by Random House, and released into the great expanse of a future, the one you and I live in. They are released to proffer their goods in a civil society, which is finally the testing ground for staying alive, is it not? To my eternal joy and surprise, only one of the men has returned to prison, which I attribute to the unspoken: something else took place in the workshop. In my words: they learn to give one another their humanity back. In their words: they learn to tolerate my insistence that they do so. Maybe then, this isn't a poetry workshop after all, but a long-standing Tuesday afternoon tea in which the things that are shared become phosphorous and lead them to discover not just art, but the sinister and the surreal that make art so necessary. If it is none of these things, that is just fine. They have permission to release the wellspring of their sorrow and reclaim the singular tenet of their existence: human value. Here, perhaps, is the membrane through which the men pass, the moment in which poetry and staying alive become synonymous. To my further astonishment, most of the men no longer write, even those who skirted with minor literary fame, which only confirms the words have done their job: they charted the way out of prison. Maybe that's reason enough to write a poem that refuses to apologize for being vulnerable to cancer, to lockdown, to the hole, to the decades-old tradition of squeezing love from the portal of desperation. Maybe that is reason enough to hold out hope for poetry and poet alike and to return each December to invoke the tradition of "A Child's Christmas in Wales." In that same tradition, they thank him with their undivided attention and return to the yard, confirmed in their desire to write what must be written.

CHAPTER ELEVEN

Trying to Answer His Question

Thanksgiving, 1990. Jess is in our Virginia City kitchen again. "I'm going in for a CT scan next week. The doctors can't tell me what's causing the headaches. I'm sure it's probably stress from the damn job." Debby and I laughed. The damn job—he was the special education coordinator for the district. What could be so bad about that? Jess had found his rhythm in South Tahoe. After the first year he moved into a two-story A-frame house—it was almost big enough for the junk that filled every room, which I took great pleasure in pointing out. "What is this stuff in your bathroom?" By turns, it could be dusty fishing rods, old magazines, fishing lures, nylon, waders, gloves, skis, or magically, a smoker with a toothbrush on top. The counters were just as dirty as they were in Redding except he was in the pines. "Why don't you come sailing with me?"

"Sailing? I can barely keep up with *my* job, let alone drive to South Shore for sailing lessons." That didn't last long. The Hobie Cat was just big enough for the two of us. Most of the time he manned the rudder while I tried to dodge the jib. When the wind came up as it invariably did in the late afternoon, he just got happier. "Maybe we can make it to Emerald Bay and back."

"Why not try North Shore?" I snapped. After the obligatory rollover, I suggested it might be time to return to the dock. "Just getting warmed up," he snorted.

"I like to feel the blood in my toes."

At home, he stir-fried smoked trout, snow peas, onions, and garlic. Jess was a minor chef. I sat in his kitchen, the sun going down, and marveled at his ability to make something taste so good. We ate with chopsticks and drank tall Sapporos. It made me think of the lone sushi bar in Redding. There were two chefs, fluent in Japanese, and Jess asked which was freshest—the maguro or the uni—and then proudly ordered what had been flown in the day before. More than once we met at that sushi bar—another island far from the island of his family. It was sanctuary. We said very little except to notice the occasional glance from a woman. Something private was held between us, something shared at the small counter with the fish in view.

There were a few good sushi bars in South Tahoe. We liked the one with the floating mats. Each time they came around you could choose what looked most interesting. Jess went there because the fish was fresh and the chefs knew how to cut and serve it. His admiration of perfection was second only to his desire to achieve it. Something neither of us will outlive. This, too, is the reign of fathers—that longing for understanding, that thrill of learning, that need for mastery and yet, it was because we cut time away from our lives to sit and talk and drink Sapporo that we could imagine a respite from the past.

Nevada sat next to us, playing with the food. For him, sushi was a mountain of Legos except they would not go together. Debby had driven up to meet us for dinner. We ate in silence and drove back to his A-frame. It was dark inside, the lone light hung from the beam above. "Can I get you something before the drive home?" Nevada fell asleep on the floor of his house. Jess looked at him and said, "You're very lucky."

Coming over Spooner Summit, I realized we had done what we wanted—moved to this beautiful place, made a living, and now, were starting a family. It had been over a decade since we left our families in Southern California. I was close to those I loved and close to the mountains. We had begun to make a home here, a home in the Sierra Nevada.

*   *   *

I was sitting by the fire and the phone rang. It was Jess's father. I was startled because I couldn't recall his ever calling me. We had talked over the years but this was new. His questions were like mountains before me: "What did the doctor tell you? When will the chemo start? Jess won't tell me what's going on." For more than thirty minutes I tried to find answers, tried to see his face in the dark. But my answers were like vapors and soon I was back to the beginning with the anguish that brought them on. I had never heard a father so distraught. "Isn't there something you can *do*?"

I listened and listened to the voice that wanted his son to be as he knew him: vital, strong, and stubborn, not as he was—somehow thinned by the seriousness of this disease. "The doctor doesn't know what else he can do. He might refer him to UC-San Francisco for surgery," I said as if that answered his question, his question that could never be answered. I didn't want to tell him any more. What could I say? That I held his son while the black fluid drained from his lungs, his body limp in my arms, and that his doctor, as strong and smart as he was, did not know what else he could do? What could I share that would calm him, would stop this dirty trick that found its way to his life? What could I offer but the minuscule prayer of my presence? "I will not leave him, I promise. If I have to drive up there every night I will."

Other nights it was his sister, Linda, her husband, Jeff, or his mother, Yoshiye, all of them living without answers. Because they lived eight hours from him, I became the interpreter, the person responsible for the knowledge, the translator of the good and the unspoken, what could only be inferred: why now, why at this time in his life when he was finally happy? Although they visited as often as they could, each visit became more intense, more worrisome. The onset of adenocarcinoma in adult men is rare. It usually occurred in young people. Jess was a grown man. Why him?

It was March and I took the afternoon off to see Jess. He was resting in bed. He had taken a leave of absence from his job. He was swollen from the chemo and radiation and did not want to eat. I was frustrated—I'd spent all morning trying to write a grant and could not get it right. I must have ranted for twenty minutes when he looked up at me and said, "I'd give anything to write a grant." Then I realized I knew nothing of what he was experiencing, too absorbed in my own confusing day to listen, to see him for what he was: my best friend, confidant, eternal wizard of facts and figures, a polecat who took me to places I never would have gone. I apologized and asked if I could bring some tea. There were flowers on the table. Some friends poked their heads in the door while we visited, and others tried to cheer him and rushed back to their lives just as I had rushed from mine. It is the curious fear of cancer that keeps people from comforting those they love. When I crested the ridge at Spooner Summit, I knew I had to get him out of that house before he could no longer travel. Maybe I could convince him to fish in Baja California. We had spent many weeks on that dry peninsula and perhaps, I naively thought, it would bring him some peace.

I called his boss when I got home. Rich was dismayed, did not know what to say except to love him through this. Rich lost his wife to cancer at twenty-eight. This was not something new to him. He had two young boys and was just starting his career as an educator. I was grateful he understood, grateful that in these mountains, Jess was not alone. He came by regularly and arranged for friends to cook his food, wash his clothes, and bathe him. His house began to look like it was stuck in slow motion: the tabletops and chairs collected small gifts, cards, and blankets from his mother. Jess was always cold.

*   *   *

I called the UCSF hospital repeatedly. Jess had been in surgery for more than eight hours. I had no way of knowing if I could get through but I had to try. I had to know what happened. "Did you get it all?" I asked plaintively.

"Almost all of it. There were a few areas I could not remove because of the proximity to cortical function."

"Almost all of it," I repeated, like it was a way to bend this tumor from the man. "What does that mean?"

"We won't know for a few months. He'll have to come back to determine if it has metastasized in other areas of the body."

These words, these words that have a punishing effect. Do you mean you do not know if it will grow again? Do you mean he may not live? Do you mean there is little more to say?

Obviously exhausted, I thanked the surgeon and hung up without knowing what to believe, what to hope for, what to report. Most unsettling, his family would arrive to this news, this news that had no recourse except to wait. When he was able to travel, Jess's family brought him back to South Tahoe.

I could report nothing to Jess that would save him from the quiet of his father's eyes. When I got to the South Tahoe hospital Jess was in tears, trying to dislodge the bone from his throat: "My father was here. He spent the morning with me. All he wanted was a healthy son. I couldn't even give him that." There was no topo map to trace the thin lines of disappointment in his voice. They were close, concentrated like those of the Sierra ridges. All at once, the silence became a sieve through which we spoke. Maybe then I understood what he was really doing— maybe he was returning to that place we had been before, high above the valley where his parents once lived. All at once language seemed useless, a point of no departure, and I placed my hands on his. There was nothing left to disturb. The nurses knew what we were trying to say. They left us in the tunnel of listless things.

Naturally, I wanted to steal time for Jess, give him the gift of distraction at this late moment. All I could think of was fishing. After repeated conversations with his family, and discreet inquiries when Jess and I were alone, he assured me he could travel. He could still walk, albeit slowly, and if the trip were relatively painless, he wanted to go. A friend was a pilot and he offered to fly us down for gas money. My parents had retired and were living on a boat in La Paz, Baja California. For hours we followed the Baja shoreline until Wayne set the small plane down. We tossed our bags to the ground and helped Jess from the plane, then grabbed the fishing gear. I had spent many afternoons in the sporting goods store before settling on a deep-sea rod and reel, line and lures, but inevitably they met with Jess's scrutiny. "I can't use this. It's for deep water trolling, not marlin, not here." I tried to protest but he could barely get up the three stairs from his room. Something in his eyes cut the morning light before I could respond.

My parents watched from the bow but could do nothing to waive off his struggle. It was late spring, close to my mother's birthday and I went to find some mariachis to sing to her from the pier. My parents had wanted to be in Mexico for most of the last decade. Now they were. It was dark when the music started and we held our margaritas high but I think Jess was afraid to hold anything for fear it might never return.

Wayne flew at low elevation on the flight home. We saw cactus and frigate birds, and the blue-green water was untouched. There was a sailboat in a cove but little more. It was the last outpost of the wild in northern Baja. I thought of Steinbeck's *The Log from the Sea of Cortez*, a book I read and reread, foolishly thinking that Ed Ricketts was like Jess, the master of the biological world. Steinbeck named the beauty in the Sea of Cortez, the life below the surface, but I could not name one shard of the indifference that lay ahead. I returned to my parent's boat months later and read *Desert Solitaire* on the back deck. My father had killed the engine. There was no breeze to lift the occasional cormorant overhead. Abbey and Steinbeck—writers we think of in the West, writers who said what this place is, but I read them for consolation, read them to understand what was missing.

*   *   *

Jess was lying in bed at the Wesners' house, the whine of oxygen pulsing from the machine to his nose. He could no longer care for himself. They gave him the room facing the east, the room with the most light in it. Friends took turns at his bedside: Ben, Karen, Debby, and myself. Others visited. It was quiet, and if there could be any peace in the days that lay ahead, it was in this sanctuary, this place where death, for a moment, could not enter. After work, I sat with him on a Friday night. It was Bob Dylan's fiftieth birthday and the local public radio host played bootleg Dylan for three hours. At last a smile came to his face. If no medical personnel could deliver a cure, there was solace in the radio waves: Jess's most cantankerous troubadour was on the prowl. I liked to imagine Jess was in the room when some of that music was recorded. At any rate, he knew it well it enough to lead us to believe its every sonic detail. Had I known it would bring this much peace to him, I would have asked the DJ to play Jackson Browne, Joni Mitchell, Bonnie Raitt, the Dead, and the Boss. Had I known this, I would have given the DJ all of my bootleg tapes that Jess made for me so that I might have music in these badlands. Had I known this, I might have asked the DJ to play the righteous radio waves all night to drown out the oxygen machine.

When I left he was asleep and there was no pain in his face. I know his presence in the Wesners' house was not easy but night and day they kept him in relative comfort. Their house was a gift of so much more than shelter. It was a place of calm with people who stopped the noise in their lives to listen, pay attention and bring simple things like water and fruit. Ben and Karen knew Jess could go any time but still they gave him permission to live without the insult of a hospital room, permission to be held and loved in his swollen, slowing state.

After three weeks in their house, Jess's family was desperate to be with him. He and I flew once again, to Southern California. I was worried he wouldn't make it, that something would happen on the plane only a doctor could handle. There was an elderly German couple in our seats and we waited in the aisle for them to relocate. The passengers looked away and Jess tried to shoulder the unwanted attention. I had asked for seats near the bathroom, not knowing what the flight would do to his stomach. When we finally sat, the oxygen bottle at our side, I prayed to God in the clouds overhead that the flight might land in Orange County with my friend alive at my side.

*   *   *

In spring we gathered on the east shore of Lake Tahoe. An Episcopal priest led the service for Jess. Most of his friends and family were there except Big Joe who didn't have enough money to drive down. Joe made it out of the hospital and he didn't know why. More than once he asked, "Why me and not Jess?" a riddle neither of us could answer but his wife and children understood. They knew a husband and father returned home. And they knew this every day.

When I called the priest to ask if he would be willing to lead us in a reading of poems and prayers for an unapologetic atheist he said, "Sure, many of my friends are former Buddhists, Wiccans, and unbelievers." I told the priest he might have been a Buddhist but I wasn't sure. What all of us wanted was someone who could let him go without judgment. I remember each of us in a circle, the sun warming the sand. Rich looked out on the lake and said how much Jess had made him laugh. Ben and Karen were grateful to have spent his last days with him. Debby talked about what a father he had already been to our boys, even though Cody was barely two years old. I read a poem to him. Jess was forty when he pulled out of the circle. The priest helped us to understand that his obdurate presence in our lives was time beyond the ordinary and we shared in it, as we share in it now.

Months after Jess died, his second nephew, Cameron, was born and I believe that his birth gave the family strength to continue on. This is what I rely on when I look at Jess's face on my dresser, his nephew's wallet photo stuffed in the corner of the picture frame. I look at him and ask what could have I done? Is there something I missed?

Sometimes Joe will call, tell me that his radio waves fade in and out from the radiation, and we talk about Jess, talk about him in the present tense because it is the only way to leave a friend—fishing, cranking the Evinrudes to an even plane, and then the inevitable tug on the line.

Episcopal Church, Virginia City, site of Shaun and
Debby's wedding, 1981
by Shaun Griffin

Red Garter Saloon, Virginia City, site of Shaun and
Debby's wedding reception, 1981
by Shaun Griffin

I Street Griffin house, Virginia City, 1981
by Shaun Griffin

I Street Griffin house in heavy snow, 1982
by Shaun Griffin

Lisa Hixson, standing by her Carson City house, 1983
by Debby Loesch-Griffin

Nevada's blessing ceremony, front of Presbyterian Church, Virginia City,
from left, Karen Wesner, Ben Wesner, Lisa Hixson, Barbara Barnhart,
Jess Hayashi, Debby, Shaun, Nevada, Bruce Bennett, Carolyn Mann,
Joe Scuncio, Andrea Whittaker, 1983
by Howard Bennett

Jess and Nevada standing by Sand Harbor, Lake Tahoe, 1986
by Shaun Griffin

First Community Chest office, C Street, Virginia City, 1991
by Shaun Griffin

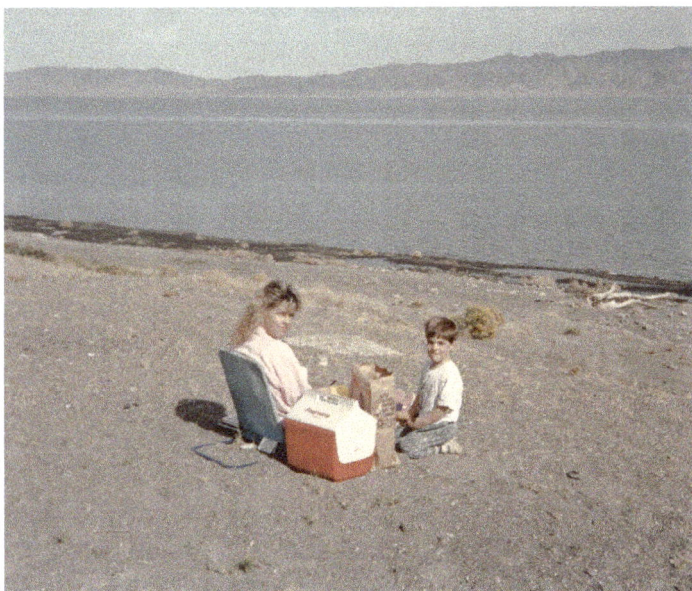

Debby and Cody at Pyramid Lake, 1992
by Shaun Griffin

Shaun and Cody atop Mammoth Mountain spreading Jess's ashes, 1992
by Debby Loesch-Griffin

II

CHAPTER TWELVE

A Mountain Schoolhouse

Billy Varga drove down the wrong side of D Street, grabbed his daughter by the nape of her neck, and jumped out of the Blazer into Virginia City Elementary School. I was almost in the school with my son. "Morning," I said.

"What—?" He never looked up from his miner's hat with the broken lamp.

"How are you?"

"Waaahhhttt—?"

"It's all right Billy. I'll see you inside."

"Here's the kid," he says to no one in particular, like he's handing off a football, turns for the Blazer, grabs the beer from the door and drives off. A little early, I think, but hey, maybe he's got a reason to meet the high-octane goddess at this hour. The bottle of Jack is lying just below his knees. Mining's been down for some time (this is before gold is rediscovered... again), and there's little work for a man like Billy. There may be little work at any time for Billy. If you make him mad, he could go off, like the mountain of explosives that took his house down some years later.

I was sitting at home, reading I think, when this horrible sound came from the rooftops on B Street. I thought it was an earthquake: this is it, this is when we drop to China or the bottom of the Sutro Tunnel. Maybe we'll end up in darkest Dayton. Maybe the daylight will be a shaft through which I crawl to my own salvation. Maybe the town will burn again. The smoke rose in puffs of black, gray and white to circle high overhead. I thought sure our little place had come to an end. The siren wailed from the courthouse. My neighbor, the volunteer fire chief, sped out of his driveway. Something was really wrong. How is it a man comes to stockpile his house with enough dynamite to level a quarter block?

Billy was nowhere to be found when it blew. He didn't even know it blew for a couple days. Scared the hell out of the neighbors, one of whom used to work for us. She and her daughter were sitting in the kitchen when Armageddon came to the Comstock. In the parlance of mining, one explosion begets another and soon the next one rang out, and the next one, until finally the house lay in smolders and the street was awash in ash and dirty water. His neighbor, a somewhat high-strung person to begin with, became even more agitated when the dynamite went off. Nothing she could do would bring normalcy back to the kitchen window. Every time she looked, she saw Billy, working, tampering, trying to fix his Chevy Blazer, trying to find what was left of his life, until in a fit of desperation, she put tar paper over the window on the south side of the house, cursed it and crossed herself so that the tattoo on her breast was rightfully protected from harm. Billy would never be seen from her kitchen window again.

He could have this effect on people: when he launched his daughter in the general direction of the school, the teachers just smiled as if he had a stick of dynamite lying next to the JD in the Blazer. This is before they knew of course but later, when the house blew, I was thankful for their contrition. Most people were thankful the whole town didn't blow, and some say Billy was in an ore car, miles below the earth, lamp flickering overhead when the deed was done. Billy didn't belong to this century. He was pissed that he came too late—the 1800s were just right: no taxes, no laws, no women—save his wild counterparts who thought a man with a gun was man enough for them. An outlaw in an ore car. This is the part of the

Comstock that gets left out of the tourist brochures. Now they hire make-believe gun fighters to torment the tourist train that smokes a diesel plume to Gold Hill, but Billy is ephemeral. He still groans beneath the earth of this town, honeycombed with timber shafts and water. Billy who came into the wrong century. Billy who thinks his time has run out. Billy whose gray Chevy Blazer should be in the Harrah's classic car collection, the oversized tires chinked with mud, the feral eyes at the wheel, the man for whom patience is a vile disease.

I like Billy. I like the fact that he won't give up despite all indicators to the contrary: lawyers, ex-wives, sheriffs from three counties, and oh yes, the threat of death from the last unarmed man he leveled in a bar. Something about Billy keeps the Comstock on edge, helps us remember who came before us, helps us reconcile the unruly with the ruled. Billy could be on a postage stamp but only if he could take his JD with him to the ceremony commemorating the lost art of staying alive underground. I haven't seen Billy for some time. Could be cancer, more likely cirrhosis, more likely still, a woman. But Billy is probably alive—the obits are always vague—no one saw him leave. No one is sure what happened. He was just gone one day, like his house. The Blazer sat in the yard for a long time, then it left too. Probably an ex sold it to the wrecking yard for child support.

And then, there's the other kind of life—the story of Billy where he's as vital as an axe. Even my old friend Donovan doesn't hold a room like Billy. When someone starts telling a Billy Varga story, he storms right in, hard hat on, cigarette in his ear and belly hanging from his pants. There he is, half in the spirit-world, half looking to come back to this one. I give thanks for men like Billy—he lets me know it's all right on the other side with all those explosives, all that heat bubbling from the inferno. I try not to forget what an incendiary gift he is: any day now this whole place could blow. I could lose everything: books, paper, even respect, but Billy pulls through, laughing, smoke-faced, saying "Whaaattt, what you want from me? Are you outta your mind? Ain't no miner worth a shit down here. Just a bunch of fucking pansies scooping rocks from a bucket." Somehow Billy survives every telling of this tale and they still won't build on the dirt lot where his house once was. No one would dare put a stake in the ground. The ghost of Billy Varga would show up at the table every night and make those owners pray to the god of things below: "You see this table? This was my table. This floor? This was my floor. This wall? This is the wall I blew down." Billy hunched in the corner, waiting for the guests to leave, waiting to start the Blazer, flick a cigarette and drive off. I'm pretty sure that lot's been de-annexed from the assessor's map. There's something in the ground, something awful in the ground, and it just won't let go.

*   *   *

The trip to school was always more interesting with Billy around—I never knew who would fall out of the cab or what odor would grace the curb. Some days I wanted to get in the back of the Blazer and see where it took me. Maybe he did have a special hole in the ground that none of us could see—a way into the earth that set him loose. Maybe it was right below the place where the principal's T-bird was sucked into oblivion. I had dropped Nevada off to school and returned home to go to work. About ten that morning he was on the playground when this giant sucking sound came from the street. He was standing by the fence, unsure of what he was seeing, and it grew louder and louder, like an avalanche of asphalt and steel and water until the T-bird convulsed in a giant brown sludge and slipped from view. At seven years old you can imagine what was going through his head: maybe it's an earthquake, maybe it's an underground river, maybe it's a giant Gila monster sucking the car from view. The kids lined up at the fence, and the teachers tried to calm them: "It's nothing, it's *just* a hole in the ground. They'll cover it up. You watch." Periodically, it would continue to convulse—this gaping hole thirty feet from the entrance to the school. The town siren wailed again and nearly every officious body but the United States Air Force swooped down. But I knew what was wrong—it was Billy in his ore car having some fun with the principal's T-bird.

My son, meanwhile, was terrified. Nothing the teachers could say assuaged him. Every day he and the other hundred or so kids were reminded: this was how it was going to end—they would be swallowed, consumed by something larger than they had ever seen. Something very destructive was in the earth.

Sinkholes are a commonplace on the Comstock—they start small, a ripple in the pavement, and then a burgeoning crater, some deeper than others. There were a couple of them on the tennis courts and just as fast, the county plugged them up. But this time was different: there hadn't been a gusher like this one in some time. This time it swallowed a car. That was a lot of water and mud and the theories flew: for weeks there were panels and presentations and many an engineer tried to explain the hole away. Billy was down low, hunkered in an ore car, laughing in the darkness. As it turns out, there was a competition among the engineers about how to plug it up. You couldn't just bury this hole with rocks and debris; this would take a bona fide system of grids and steel and mesh—an oversized cork that would be stuffed into the hole. This took some engineering. Of course, no one really knew what to do. There hadn't been a sinkhole like this in thirty years. So it was speculation: this system may work; it's the best we can design; it's nearly foolproof, and so on. Like making a bridge with imaginary foundations. The road was blocked off for months and the principal's brand new yellow T-bird was never seen again. Billy's probably under the hood, tinkering with it right now, trying to get it on the ore tracks, hoping for a miracle of conversion.

Going to school became a real event: the cranes came, the steel girders, the mesh piles, and every day dozens of men dressed in hard hats studied the hole: would it continue to grow, would it turn out like the last one—an idle conversation piece, or would it expand to the edge of the school? My son was worried and so were the other kids. This could ruin the playground, make school really boring. They could no longer watch it grow from the fence—it may open up and swallow more of the street. Recess took place inside, which was pretty awful. You can only run so far in the music room. Of course we were assured nothing more would really happen— the water had done its damage. A broken pipe was to blame: water had run into the ground for days causing the eventual slip of soil beneath the street. But to a resident for whom sinkholes are almost normal, this is like saying the Hindenburg won't crash again. Some things just can't be explained away.

Faith has its purpose and as I listened to the engineers explain the solution, I knew theirs must be very strong. This was not something subtle, this was not remodeling your kitchen. There was of course, the real question: when would the hole swallow the school?

To which the engineers could only surmise: unlikely, very unlikely. To the parents, the children, and the town fathers, it was nevertheless possible and to a person, protections were taken: alternate routes to school, emergency escape drills, and articles on what to do if your street swallowed a car. Every place has its peculiar requirements for being there—weather, bugs, and isolation—but the earth giving way was a challenge for even the most hardy.

There's probably a hundred open mine shafts on the Comstock and some, no doubt, are the choice of last resort for the wild horse killed on the highway or the uncooked pig we barbequed for twenty four hours underground. While deadly if fallen into, they can serve a purpose: they consume what isn't wanted. But this was different: had there been a child in front of the school that day, they might not have returned home. This forced us to re-examine our certainties: is the street in front of the school really a street, is the steel plug really going to hold up under the first rain or snow storm, will the street buckle under the weight of the first school bus or trash truck, will the next vehicle be even bigger? Some things just don't have answers and so we trusted the hard hats to do their jobs. Next to the forces that sucked that T-bird from view, Billy looked tame. Maybe that's the way he wanted it: something to outlive his reputation, something of truly grand proportions on the Comstock.

The lengths we'll go to make things safe: now the street is paved, the buses stop, and the kids march into the hallway. Rhythm has returned to the school day. Even I trust the surface to walk my dog after work. Newcomers question if it ever happened. But Billy knows, my son knows, and the principal drives a shiny new T-bird in the valley below. She transferred the following year reasoning, if you have to work, it may as well be on solid ground. This, of course, defies the local logic: if you live over a mountain of decaying mine shafts, there's bound to be some excitement.

*　　　　　　*　　　　　　*

Maybe I had to get past Billy and the T-bird before I could say anything about the music, before I could remember "Taps" playing in the street and the hundreds of people gathered outside the mountain schoolhouse. It was one of those bright gorgeous mornings on the Comstock and there were men in uniform, friends and family, and all of the students around the podium. Teachers were crying. We wanted to know why, why the music teacher went in the mine. He was a prankster and something drew him in—the risk of getting out alive, the ordinary thrill of dodging death—I'm not sure. What I do know is that he gave the kids more music than they knew what to do with. Horns, drums, flutes, guitar, cymbals and a chance to play them. A young father of twins, he wanted his students to play music like they were on top of Mt. Davidson giving a dress rehearsal to every ear for a hundred miles. And that's what they did—every day in the band room. Nevada took up French horn, trumpet, and later, piano. Each sound was like new bird flying around the house. Sometimes the bird hit the glass and we had to duck for cover but the birds were part of something larger, something that swept into the mountain schoolhouse and brought each child the opportunity to make sounds that slowly became music. He taught them to get out of the way, to let go and play like the angels they were. Miraculously, every year when he held the spring concert, it worked. It was like going to a performance of fifty starlings, huddled on the stage in a cacophony of squeaks, starts, stops, burps, and claps before their conductor. They heard rhythm, harmony, a sound coming from the instrument in their hands and it gave them permission to make more sounds. It gave them a belief in what could be heard with a little practice. But he never used that word. Not once did he admonish our son to sit down and play. This was his gift: music was a way out of this world, it freed them to make an entirely different sound, something they had never imagined. It was like having a new voice—one that felt good to be sharing. Once his students heard it they wanted more. They wanted to be a starling in the treetops. They wanted to make music no one had heard.

That's why we were crying in front of the schoolhouse. No teacher had made an orchestra of noisy instruments or asked the children to play in one. No teacher had shown them how to sound like starlings or listened to their every mistake as if it was breath. No teacher had led them to top of Mt. Davidson to play for an entire desert, even if it was in the portable music classroom. No teacher had witnessed the birth of their unwieldy sounds and now that first explorer in their lives was gone. Suddenly the instruments became weighted and what was once playful, took on the aura of homework. The music in the mountain schoolhouse faded from view. We feared the program would die and the music never return.

That's when she walked in—the woman who climbed mountains and traveled to exotic places. The woman who studied music at a prestigious college, the woman who was strong enough to let people mourn the loss of their teacher and still move out of his shadow. The woman who was in the *Guinness Book of World Records* for playing over 1,800 songs from *memory*. That's when Squeek walked in.

She had a piano in her house and almost every student who ever thought of playing it came to her for instruction. She was particularly good at ragtime. Her husband recorded the music and they sold it through the mail. The first day she came to class with her giant Walking Piano the kids knew it was going to be all right: you could walk on the piano, play it with your feet, learn entire scales by stepping on the keys. This was pretty cool. Only a woman who had been up Kilimanjaro could walk across the room on a piano.

Like most kids in the town, both of our sons went to her for instruction. The inside of her house was a prism to another era: soft lights, kerosene heaters, a poster of Houdini on the wall, and coal embers in the wood stove. Nothing was modern except the recording equipment. They found a way to restore an antique stove and refrigerator, to refurbish the iron bed and the bear claw tub. At the front of the house was her piano. I left work early to listen to her teach the kids. They were in awe of her—she knew exactly what to do to draw them out. At recitals even the most timid student performed. If they didn't come back to it for fifteen years they remembered her: at a local punk rock concert the bass guitarist was happiest when Squeek showed up. And it was she who threw her head back in elation when he set his guitar down to begin improvising at the piano. Variations on a riff from childhood.

Like the time I walked in to watch her teach Cody Beethoven's "Ninth." He started through the motions and she vaulted up: "Not like that! Like *this!*" and pounded on the keys: *dhon-dhon-dhon-dhaaa* because that's how Cody lived in the world—tactilely, with emphasis. She opened the symphony up to him through his body— he could feel the force of that sound reverberate and knew it was powerful, almost intoxicating. It was something to emulate, a way to express emotion, and that was a profound discovery for him. He learned that classical music would never lie down. It was a sonic leap into the air and he could turn it on when most needed.

In the mornings when I awoke, Cody was downstairs practicing the music she had given him the week before. The concentration on his face grew with each repetition. It was like he was balanced above the keys, trying to adjust his fingers for the precise touch. I sat in the kitchen and listened. Snow was falling. There was little sound except the piano and Cody focused on the parallel keys. Off we drifted to the winter morning. He wanted to play baseball but the snow wouldn't let up and so the piano became his refuge, became our refuge. Even though he would never say it was jazz he was playing, as he learned to manipulate the keys, the internal rhythm of a chord, my affection for this time grew deeper and deeper. Yes, the snow would not stop and yes, it would be another month before the first pitch, but I was already at peace in my kitchen: my son was sitting at the piano, jazz was in the house.

CHAPTER THIRTEEN

The Soprano Behind the Plate

Little League is neither little nor a league. The parents are a nefarious group of sidewinders looking for someone to strike—which happens to be other parents. Debby and I endured eight seasons in the frigid springs of northern Nevada, something like sitting in the bleachers at a wind farm on the Arctic shelf. You could do worse, but I'm not sure where. The greatest irony of baseball is that everyone thinks they can play and that is the first rule in Little League: they can. So—entire innings go by with the little ones picking dandelions in the outfield grass, drawing pictures on the infield sand, herding the rabbits from the dugout, and running, usually as fast as they can, to the outhouse. There's rarely any time for the game, because the game is getting all of the kids to pay attention long enough to begin. It's usually about then that the first parent speaks up—"Why can't you coach, you idiot?"

Uh, me, the guy who just got off work, ran to the sporting goods store and dropped $50 on a mitt? Nah, that couldn't be me you were talking to. Must be my neighbor, one of the other volunteers too foolish to say no, which I take great comfort in, given his size. In fact both of my fellow volunteers are big and both are relatively secure in the presence of parents—through the first three innings. There are only minor transgressions until the third inning. By then, one team is ahead forty-to-one, and inevitably their child is on the losing team. They feel like it is their right to protest every call, every possible nuance of choice ("Why didn't you pitch my kid, you idiot?"—twice in the same game, a new high). And so it begins: the three of us try to negotiate the flying duty hazards—paper cups, peanuts, and the Gatorade box floating in the wind—and the subtle parents in the stands: "He can pitch better than that jerk." By the fifth inning, which is one from the last, the dust has accumulated in most of our pores and our eyes begin to close out of preservation:

"No, I didn't see the f...ing strike. I was trying to avoid dying from sand blindness. Would you like to umpire?"

"You call one more outside and I'll—"

"Switch places—?"

"With your f...ing idiot self?" Three times—a new record.

Yes, it's a lovely day for baseball. When the game's over we go the pizza joint and order enough beer to survive the critical question: how long before we have to play *them* again. The kids, of course, play for one reason—pizza—which, as rewards go, is not so bad. You can eat cheese and pepperoni for most of your twenties, maybe into your thirties, before the Little League curse catches up with you and you will have to return to the dugout, an unwilling volunteer, except it will be with a few extra pounds. Then, suddenly, it will all look very different: why are they picking on me? I haven't even chosen the lineup yet, and half the parents have called me out for ignoring their son or daughter—which keeps moms in the crowd and dads from becoming garden-variety vigilantes. Here's the catch—if you don't coach, they will—meaning your admirers in the stands. Welcome to the 1 X 12 bench in the brick and chain link sanctuary. Coaching isn't so bad as long as you can avoid leaving the dugout. As long as you can out-yell your opponents, there's a reasonable chance of reversing a few bad calls.

What they don't tell you when you sign up is that one coach from each team must umpire. Being the skinny guy and the smallest of the three, I was selected after careful consideration: you're even-tempered Shaun. You'll be fine. You don't want *me* out there. You know what I'll do if one of those parents get in my face. You don't want *me* either—it's pretty stressful behind the plate and I might smack 'em. I think you should do it. It's nothing really—just watch the ball and make the call. Half the time the kids don't even see the pitch—you gotta' remind 'em to swing.

It required apparatus—a strike counter, facemask, and a white hand brush to clean the plate. The rulebook I could never remember, much less the count. Sometimes I forgot to advance the strike counter but I was frequently reminded: "You idiot—can't you see that was a ball!" Four times—I'm going to break my old record. Needless to say, a coach from each team took turns behind the plate when the opponent was up. In the great mythology of Little League, this prevented us from any strategic advantage: we couldn't call our son or daughter safe, couldn't give them the benefit of the doubt when the pitch was close. As mentioned, decorum lasted until the third inning when it was becoming obvious their son or daughter was on the losing team—"Hey, four eyes, get a clue," or my favorite, "Can't you count to three?"—which normally required I turn my head and try to spot the one pair of eyes in the stands who might have said this. Somehow they disappeared from view. Not one person had the slightest clue who might have called me out. After it escalated in the fifth— "Your momma must have had you in the backseat of a Chevy—" I casually walked to the fence that separated us—"If I hear that again, you're out of here." It never worked. Even with my big volunteer neighbors in the dugout.

One afternoon they were going to call the game when no one could umpire on the other team. I volunteered, thinking that my sons wanted to play more than eat pizza, but only after I told my fellow coaches: if I make a bad call you cannot disagree with me. If I call your son out, so be it. I will try to be fair, but I don't want to be argued with.

"No problem, Shaun, we got your back."

Somehow I knew this wouldn't end well. I should have resigned from coaching that afternoon, should have said farewell to fairness, to the obligatory discussion of good sportsmanship, and driven straight to the pizza joint. It was another windless afternoon— this was important: the field was dirt. After hundreds of little feet pounding it for weeks on end, it was now closer to silt. When the wind blew, no one could see. The game was slow—pizza began to look better in the bottom of the third. But today, our team was on the verge of winning. We needed one more run to make it happen. The tallest kid on our team was up. He whiffed a few times and then connected for a double. After a single he slid into third. The parents were screaming. My fellow coaches were hardly audible, even though one of their sons was on third. The next batter hit a single into the outfield and the kid on third ran as hard as he could. The left fielder threw the ball to home plate, and the next thing I knew all of us were rolling in a dust cloud. I stood up and tried to remember what happened. There was ominous quiet—"He's out." My friend stormed from our dugout and I thought I was gonna die. "He's not out, you idiot!" Five times—this surely will be on my headstone.

"I don't care what you saw. I'm not changing my call."

"You lame little asshole!"

The other team was watching to see who would win. I didn't let on—in fact I didn't think about anything. But I knew—right or wrong—I had to stay with my call. We lost the game and the pizza was lousy. But I learned that Little League can be just as serious as hostage negotiation.

This was in full view a few seasons later when our son's coach decided to pick up his chair and leave the game. There was no adult in the dugout. Not one. The kids were looking at each other: are you up next? I don't know, where's the line-up card? You were out last— it's my turn. The doting parents made a hasty recovery. We dove into the dugout in unison. The coach, it seems, was aggravated because his daughter wasn't pitching as well as she might. This was a former major leaguer, mind you. A pretty good one, but his wrath could not be calmed, and so we tried to find our way through the end of the game without a roster, without a coach.

*   *   *

Little League was prime preparation for what was to come— more sidewinders and fewer excuses: high school ball. Nevada pitched through most of Little League. He was tall, a lefty, and it was a challenge for the batter to find the pitch. In a small school in rural Nevada almost everyone plays, including two of our foreign exchange students. You also become intimately familiar with the opponents. Spring, which normally starts during snow season and ends right before the onset of habitable weather, is the period when this initiation occurs: if you thought it was cold inside, try the stands. They'll cure you of any whining. What I most appreciated about the one or two Saturdays when it was clear, was the place: Smith Valley had the best ballpark—no doubt. This was just miles from where I first came to Yerington, and driving home through Wilson Canyon to Highway 395, you could get lost looking at the raging Walker River. Their field was the first to green up because it was at a lower elevation. They watered earlier and their athletic director, who doubled as the coach, made it his project to have the field ready for spring ball. Over the years, the faces that returned—parents, kids, and grandkids—became familiar, and we began to rely on them for this ritual of meeting behind home plate. We talked about small things mostly, but there were times when the conversation was real: "How's your son? Is he in college now?" and the endless trials of the student who was kicked out for speaking his mind: "Did he ever get back into school? Did he graduate?"

Sitting in those Smith Valley stands I could wait for hours for the game to begin. Sun was everywhere, something like spring was outside, and all I wanted was a reason to stay. Maybe they'd get through the first game of the tournament, maybe we'd get called back for the tie-breaker, maybe someone would forfeit and we could play again. Debby made exotic food, but the burgers usually won out and still it didn't matter. On the way home we stopped at J & T Basque Restaurant and ate like we had played—meaning the parents. It gave us time away from our lives. This was critical. Debby and I were just beginning the second decade of Community Chest and there were many nights when the hangover from work lingered in the stands. Saturday was a reprieve. Both of us are given to working too much but we couldn't in the bleachers. All we could do was pay attention, the gift of the Buddhists. All we could do was root for our team, and root for the other team because it was a small school. Their kids were just as scrappy, as underfunded, as far from the universe of a city as our kids. It was time away from time. The drive slowed us down, the purposeful existence outside of changing a community. We never imagined it would become something we could want, we could need to disrupt us from our routine. The hardest part of living in a small town is that the work never ends but when you leave, even for a day, it does. The phone goes off, the habitual response to crisis goes away, and you wake up again—like most of the others in the stands—to the day outside: the dirt in the glove, the grass in the cleats, the sweat on the brow. I always prayed Nevada would pitch a perfect game, but he pitched best when I wasn't there. Still, it was an absolute joy to recoil with every windup, to watch with trepidation when the ump shook his fist—"Steeee-riiiike." The coaches were some of the best people he encountered in high school. The head coach had been a pitcher in college and spent a lot of time teaching Nevada how to throw. After graduation, the other coach took nine months to paint Nevada's Toyota Land Cruiser. Nevada bought the paint and his coach brought that steel back without any bonding material. He polished the metal until he could be certain every ding and dent was repaired. There was no rust on that car. None. When he finished it was teal green metal flake with white trim. It killed us to sell the car for his college tuition, but Nevada will never forget what that man did for him—out of kindness.

The painter's son would later become Cody's coach and he was every bit as strong an influence on Cody. Ironically, Cody was a catcher—a big, husky guy behind the plate. His young coach had also been a catcher, so he helped Cody with the fundamentals. After sitting through four years of pitching with Nevada, it was a whole other perspective to be watching home plate. All we could see was his back and wait for the pitcher to shake off his signs. Inevitably, Cody would start singing. Suddenly there was a voice behind the plate. Even if I had left the stands, I could hear him humming the bars of a rock and roll tune. When the game resumed he was all focus. If there was a runner on third, it looked more like football than baseball. Cody was a physical kid—no one was going to slide into home safely. When the dust rose, he was on the plate most of the time and he took great pride in saving the run. Like any catcher, his knees got sore but he could last through a double-header without complaint. He was the cocky spirit-leader on the field: "Two down"; "Play's at home"; "Get your cut-off…" and on it went into the seventh inning.

Cody taught me something else: the rhythm between catcher and pitcher. By his senior year he had caught for all of the strong arms on the team. He reassured them when they struggled to laugh off the critics in the stands. It became a relationship of innings— could they last the distance, could they save the power for the final outs, could they hold up on the away field?

Our home field was anything but: it was smaller than the others because it doubled for a softball field in the county park. There was almost no room between home plate and the backstop. This meant everyone in the stands was on their toes. This also meant the field was wet through the first half of the season—late snow, mud, and no warmth kept baseball at arm's length. The field was ready for play just about the time the season ended. For three games we had less distance to drive—it wasn't in Mark Twain or some other makeup field. Home runs came easy: for one or two afternoons each season, the kids could be heroes. It was never really a field, but they managed. Managed through countless snowstorms, wind, and practice long after the sun set. Living at the base of a mountain meant the sun went down at 4, 4:30 and so the next hour was cold and the last was real cold. But baseball was more than staying warm: it was a way for twenty kids to stay alive on the Comstock.

        *   *   *

We drove for hundreds of miles to get to a game—Wells, Jackpot, Eureka, Carlin, Coleville, and slowly began to thread the web of rural Nevada. Families, teachers, and coaches called these places home. Sometimes the stories in the stands were hard: in Silver Springs I asked a woman how she was doing. "Fine—I finish chemo in three weeks. I hope I'm here next season." Sometimes I learned to listen to the kids and let the parents go. When we differed, it was awkward to be in such close proximity. When our differences were serious it spilled into the game—petty jealousies and anger at the kids when they were just trying to play. But I felt an obligation to be with them. The weather was never predictable and the teams played through rain, dust storms, snow, and heat. How could I ask my kids to get on the bus if I wasn't willing to join them?

When work bled into the stands, small conversation was especially difficult. I wished we could be swept from the folly of a small town, wished to understand how our trivial failings could lead us to this place, this place of silence among friends. Another employee had stepped over the line and his son was on the team. I kept looking at the boys on the field—did any of this matter to them? I returned to the silence of the top row in the bleachers, tried to find the beauty in the game, in the small-town heroics of the boys on the field. It was a microcosm for so much more—our petty difficulties far beyond the field. "Something there is that doesn't love a wall" as Frost said. I understood we could not hold these grudges in perpetuity, and yet I foolishly wanted some acknowledgment of the perceived indiscretion.

I came back to the game. I could not separate my sons from their son. Call it human failing, call it what we cannot know, but their time was also time outside of time—away from the halls of high school, the books, and the make-believe sincerity. This was real, and who was I to take that from them? I was only a parent, someone who lived outside of time for the brief eight hours of a Saturday.

I grew close to many of the coaches, knew some by name, by habit. In Coleville, the coach was a man who wanted the kids to shine. That was the only reason he was on the field. Coleville was smaller than Virginia City. It was at the southern end of the valley below Topaz Lake, which was fed by the West Walker River. The cottonwoods that lined 395 were some of the oldest in the region. You could almost mistake it for rural New England. I drove that road in a furious rainstorm in my Chevy woody. I thought the wood panels would cave in from the pounding but I also thought it was one of the last untouched places on earth. Coleville had seen its share of scrapes—the kids who lost it in the middle of a game. It didn't matter what kind of game, because most of the athletes played all of the sports. We knew them, just like they knew us. I asked the coach how they were doing now that the drama of high school was over. Some were all right, some had fallen even further. Just like our kids. But he wanted to know everything about our boys, about the rest of the team. He realized baseball was simply a way to move beyond the finite walls of the classroom. It was a way for the young people to live, however briefly, outside the tedium of learning. It taught other things, and although it could be harsh and unforgiving, it brought balance to the kids' lives. They championed the small diamond of home.

In the winter we were in other bleachers—basketball—but it took us throughout the northern half of the state as well. I liked

Pyramid Lake. It brought me back to the fishing, to the edge of that beauty just north of the high school. The tribe received money to build a museum there and their new school was recently completed. It was a stark contrast to much of the reservation, a place of light beyond the darkness. We ate Indian tacos and told lies about the cutthroats we never caught and watched as each generation brought their history to the court. Families who had lived in this valley for a hundred years. Families whose great-grandchildren were playing this sport so foreign to their elders. But it was pride that brought them in the room. Pride of place, of culture, a satisfaction in seeing something mastered—this new game. Their coach was similarly a leader of the young people. The thing he wanted most was freedom from limitation—he wanted them to succeed, not just on the court, but afterwards, after they had gone home. The reservation was its own painful net and they had to find a way to live within it. We went to these games with trepidation—the old rivalries could become hardened into disgust very quickly and then they weren't so pretty. We found repose in the aisles, in the half-time show, in the music. We wanted cooler heads and sometimes we left without them.

It is a cliché to say we are different, but if we let it threaten what brought us together—our children—the game becomes a tension of cultures. I look up. The refs inflame the crowd, we stand on our feet and scream at the unwanted foul. If it drops, they win. If it doesn't we drive home in celebration. By the time we get to Nixon, there are stars overhead, a cottonwood split from its trunk lies at the turn to Wadsworth, the last town before leaving the reservation. Basketball, the phantom game that brought us together for these few hours, disappears in the mirror. Something has called us home. We drive on, leave the Truckee River Canyon to the ghost of Captain Storey.

CHAPTER FOURTEEN

The Woman and Her Children

There is little doubt that Community Chest could have thrived without Debby as its co-founder. She brought a statewide service-learning project to the office and from 1991-2000, coordinated it. This gave us much-needed cash flow and the resilience to keep growing locally when the resistance was strongest. She established herself across the state as a leader on youth issues, evaluation and facilitation, and she provided the connective tissue in our growing organization.

Still, she worried—about the effects of living in a small town on our boys and about the lack of diversity. Her time co-facilitating the desegregation project in Los Angeles schools gave her experience that, frankly, was missing from that of our boys. That is why she wanted them to know other cultures, other ways of living. It was clearly the reason for our time volunteering abroad in 2002. We lived for extended periods in South Africa and Northern Ireland so that the boys and our neighbor's daughter, Alix, who came with us, would know something other than the relative homogeneity of their mountain home.

It also was the reason we had so many exchange students. Our house became the home to students from Japan, Mexico, Argentina, Congo, and Uruguay. They felt awkward at first—out of place in this very different landscape, but in most cases, were embraced by the community and the school. Chris, our lone black student, was the brunt of more than a few slurs but he never expressed discontentment with the place or its people. The high school was very good about integrating the students. All of them did something: played sports, dated, skied, and went to the prom or other outings. Each had their special temperament which made for exciting times: Chris never had enough to eat; Leandro was boisterous and kept the boys laughing; Diego and Shoma were thankful to live in a house of relative kindness. They traveled on the bus to team sports, drove with us to special events, and when we left town, they came along. This, in turn, gave us yet another family—their families— who to this day are grateful their sons and daughters acquired English in a tiny mountain town.

Leandro couldn't sleep for the first two weeks; it was too quiet. He was raised in Buenos Aires. Marien was freezing in August. She came from a tropical climate south of Mazatlán, but once she acclimated never wore a jacket—no matter what the temperature. Shoma could not believe you could buy Levis in a thrift store; the same pants at home (outside of Tokyo) cost $200. This was the conundrum of coming to a very rural home in northern Nevada: for all of them it was completely unlike what they had left.

Marien was the closest Debby came to having a daughter— something she wanted deeply. Marien was quiet, smart, and had graduated from high school before coming here to study. She wanted to become fluent in English. It took some time to draw her out, but by spring she was at ease in our house and in the community. She grew up in a way that her parents marveled at. She became a young woman, more confident, secure, and outgoing.

Marien suggested we take Community Chest's Global Voice project to her home. For two weeks we took high school students (most from Virginia City) to participate in service-learning abroad. This was prefaced by study of the culture, the people, and the language. Her parents were educators in two small rural schools.

Our students painted the schools, taught English, built a library, playground equipment, and repaired or constructed the basketball and volleyball courts—with the students from the schools. Invariably the young people came home changed for the better. They had a broader worldview and it was made all the more real by seeing their classmates, the foreign exchange students alongside them, year in and year out. For a small school, there were always 4-5 students from other countries on campus. This made a difference in the experience of all of the students. It helped the local kids not take themselves so seriously and similarly, helped to initiate the "outsiders" into the inner circles of friendship they so desperately desired in high school.

Any time you invite people into your house it becomes smaller. Debby cooked, cleaned, and tolerated more, but felt like she was doing her part to make this very small community diverse. It is amazing to learn how much of a young person's experience is based on the few encounters with others from that time. Yet, because of having shared it with students from other nations, they claim that history, however small or personal. It was a window to another culture and it was the one through which they looked.

*　　　　　*　　　　　*

About ten years after we started Community Chest, Debby received word from Lisa, who was by then living in Hawaii. She had retired early from teaching and moved to her island sanctuary. She was battling a very large tumor. Debby wondered how this could happen: Lisa was an ardent swimmer and a fierce athlete. For years she, Barbara, and four other women took turns swimming across Lake Tahoe on the last weekend in July, hard enough in any water let alone the cold waters of that mountain lake. How was it that her best friend could be in such pain in the prime of her life? This was a question she would ask herself over and over. She wondered what alchemy had taken place to put this woman in her life, this woman with whom she built a fresh existence in this home of mountain and sage? Lisa was Debby's source of laughter, frolic, and mischief. She was fiercely independent, she took things on, leveled the playing field for women. Debby could never understand her fearlessness but she wanted to know it. She trusted her to do what was right—first with the kids at the alternative school, and later with her friends and family.

When Lisa moved to the big island of Hawaii Debby lost proximity to her best friend. She was a long-distance phone call away. She received occasional letters from her but the unspoken news was hard to glean. She couldn't meet her for dinner, go to a movie, or just sit and talk about ideas. And I couldn't rely on her teasing to keep me in line. On my love of cars—"That's so lower chakra, Shaun," and how dare I take work seriously—"Come ski with us, for god's sake!" There was levity in this woman and a profound love of our boys. She gave them every kindness—read to them, played with them, and nurtured their understanding of our roles as men and women. She was like another mother to them but not in the feminine sense; rather, she let them enjoy their raucous boyhood selves and repeatedly admonished us to lighten up. A woman any person would want in their extended family.

This is why it was so hard to countenance her slipping from the banter of her mortal frame: she was the compass of true things in the unreliable world of falsehoods and chicanery.

When we gathered by the river near her former Verdi home we lit candles, burned sage, and read poems. Her oldest Nevada friends were there—many of those same men and women who started with her at the alternative high school. I read a poem written for her but it did not account for her absence. The morning light shown through the Lombardi poplars. Lisa, although gone, was all around us. We felt her as surely as we felt the sun and tried to release her from this world. She was spiritual but not religious, and it was to that place we hoped she had gone.

Into this void of friendship lost, Debby stepped. I stepped with her trying to find a reason for such sorrow in the life of her closest companion. Again, we turned to each other, not knowing what was left to be done. Lisa would live on but not in our company: memory would construct its temple now.

*   *   *

Nevada and Cody were never sure of our whereabouts: were we at a commissioner's meeting, the school board, or just running to the next event? To their credit, they didn't complain, although they grew weary of the constant movement. This was the case since their births—the preschool grew out of our needing childcare, and so they were in the fabric of our work and play every day. It gave them a keen perspective on this community: what was here and what was not. They were the outsider's children who had to earn their own respect in what could be a parochial place—narrow attitudes, defined beliefs, and strong traditions.

Debby was constantly in the schools doing whatever it took to make their experience, and the experience of all the students, the best it could be. She challenged the school board to live up to its expectations of a well-rounded curriculum, met frequently with the administrators to help them understand things like Global Voice and the need for music and art when heretofore, sports had been the lone mantra. Both of our sons participated in sports and it gave them a great deal of satisfaction. Leandro happily rode the bench and Shoma was a strong third basemen.

When we returned from our long journey abroad, Cody's hair had grown over his ears, a seemingly innocuous event in 2003. It was not; the coach told him to cut it or he could not play basketball. He decided to snowboard instead, despite having played basketball in leather shoes on black top for the middle school outside of Cape Town, not to mention Gaelic football in the Rostrevor rain, also in leather shoes. This was when the community and the school became too small. We often wondered if we had made the right choice to live here. Had we somehow given our kids the wrong perspective? A failed perspective—the closed mind that ruled decisions such as these.

When Cody started back to high school it was the spring semester of his freshman year. He had just lived abroad for six months. He imagined that his peers would want to know everything about the trip but gave up when he was met with, "What was it like?" and then, "Gotta go." He was an anomaly in the school and felt like he didn't belong: "School was just an act to go through. So I went through the day to get home with my family who understood who I was, where I had been. I was very young, having skipped a grade, and did not have the maturity to understand my situation. My friends, I incorrectly thought, would not be able to understand what I had just done."

What gave both of the boys the desire to succeed in spite of these moments were many fine teachers. Ric Schrank, our neighbor and a serious bicyclist, was their shop teacher who became a close friend. Bob Clerico, their math teacher, was beloved by all of the students and faculty. Most of the high school faculty were singular in their commitment to their subjects and their students—and many were our friends too, Karen Kreyeski, the painter who taught art, Chris Prater, who taught Spanish, and Bert Young, who taught several youth employment students at Community Chest. This was true from the time they entered school. Some of their elementary teachers were the best we have known and gave them that initial love of learning. In middle school Barbara Bush taught them to think about math like it was food—necessary and enjoyable. She also taught them to write poetry, an unthinkable combination unless you were Ms. Bush.

School is not an endurance test; it is an opportunity to grow a mind. Getting to that agreement took constant vigilance. I have no illusions that it is better in some places and worse in others. I also know it can be better in all places.

When we were in South Africa, our kids went with us to the skeletal schools in Khayelitsha, a township outside of Cape Town. One of Cody's teacher's wives taught there. There were seventy students in the classroom. Most didn't have books; a few had pencils and paper. But they wanted to attend, they needed to be there. School represented freedom. As poor as they were, their parents paid to send them to school.

Debby and I tried to create an environment in which our boys could flourish. We tried to teach them the values of a larger world. We expected them to live with those values. I was afraid to be a father; I thought I would fail but this place allowed us to ride bikes, hike, and name what it was we lived in. We were novices and we grew up together. Our family trips into the Jarbidge wilderness are our most revered moments. The hike into Emerald Lake is about eight miles and 3,800 feet in elevation. The summit is over 10,200. On the last trip in, I chanted the poem written for the boys on an earlier hike we took together. This is the last stanza:

> I reason with the marks of work and men
> most of the year, but today, smoke-filled
> and arguably the happiest I've been, relinquish

my stern hold on things and clutter the lake
with my bones, the three of us, cold naked stones.

Just as I have no doubt Community Chest would have
floundered without Debby, I am equally certain our boys learned
to appreciate being in the Great Basin and among its people, who
cannot be reduced to summary.

CHAPTER FIFTEEN

When Jake Came Wheezing to the Door

Snow flew at the window and Sunday slowly closed to darkness. A U-Haul was at the end of the street. I couldn't imagine anyone moving in this weather, anyone but Jake. "Moving to Montana—." It was mid-December.

"Not much time to get there before the real cold comes," I hollered.

"Don't matter. I got to. This place is killing me." This place, meaning his house, had lead paint on the siding.

If that were all that's killing you, I thought.

When Jake moved in, our dog was perpetually on the loose. There was no fence or wall that could keep him. The boys showed up at his door looking for him. "I'll shoot that thing if I ever see him again." He stood in the doorway, cigarette dangling and not much dignity left to defend.

This became known as the day Jake moved in, a chronicle of unhappy events that wound themselves into this U-Haul some years later. We had found our neighbors. We just hadn't planned on finding this much of them.

*   *   *

Jake worked in construction with long hair, tattoos, and the obligatory hangover in the blaze of northern Nevada light. His hands were hard and he knew his work. He'd run his outfit for almost twenty years. But it was never quite as easy to come home and be a part of things, his family and people beyond the house like us. I don't think he stayed in one place long enough to forge a relationship with others. I never wanted to hurry things with Jake. I wondered what lurked beneath the workingman. My curiosity wasn't idle. His truck started religiously in the dark and he came home 9, 10 hours later, burnished like hard wood from bulldozing dirt and rock in a new development. I admired this—labor for his family, for his kids and grandkids that lived with him. Two of the grandkids were in school with our boys and did pretty well until high school. I wondered how long it would take before things fell apart.

It was like watching a movie in slow motion. More than once the elder daughter came screaming from the door in tears and cussed at him from the middle of the street. I stood in the back of our aging ski boat and yelled, "Are you OK?" She nodded, yes, choking up her anger. I wondered if this was going to be the moment when something else happened. Then his wife flew into the street. Again I asked, and again she nodded her head. I didn't believe either person. I couldn't believe either person. I was no stranger to torment: these women were living in fear. Minutes later Jake battled back: "You got somethin' with me? Get your fuckin' ass over here, you n-loving motherfucker."

There wasn't much to do—I didn't want it to escalate. I stood in the boat and looked for something to protect myself. This might get worse. Debby was inside and I didn't want her out of the house. If it all went south, at least it was in the street. He stood there, staring me down, looking for revenge, for something or someone to blame. I looked back and didn't have any words, straddled the engine cover, and felt nothing but fear. He yelled again and I listened but with no one to fight, the words fell flat, and he busted the gate on the way back into the house.

The n-word. I hadn't heard that in years. Somehow, race had floated into his anger at his granddaughter or me, I'm not sure. But it was clearly remonstrance for our actions: we had a foreign exchange student from the Congo living with us and that was wrong in his eyes. Without asking we had violated the code, the ideal of how you live in harmony. We had stepped too far from the idyll of this small community, and broken his trust in our ability to understand such tacit agreements. All of which stank for reasons that by now, are obvious. Did I have any recourse? I reasoned not except to live on with our student, our sons and their friends who came to the house. This was a fault line and I had crossed it. The traces of intolerance had crept to our little perch on the edge of a mountain. This is when a community becomes something larger than living together, something that most of us try to avoid—a confrontation. This is when the households tilt with the vehemence of their residents.

Jake's house was beaten from years of weather, and it was never built right in the first place. On Saturdays, he'd nail the shingles down after another hard wind. He replaced the flu pipe and anchored it with guy-wires to keep it from sailing to the bottom of Six Mile Canyon. He planted an Austrian pine, a birch, a lawn, and flowers. He mended the land that was never intended to be a garden. There was pride in that small green patch, an element of honor that broke still more of the boundaries of neighborliness. This was what he had. He would make of it what he could. When he mowed his lawn, it was an affirmation that something was right in the yard. I borrowed his mower on occasion, when mine broke or just wouldn't start. I did this to transgress the silence, to find a way back to living nearby before the violence and the anger started.

He worked with things like a bee in a hive. If the three-wheeler found on the job didn't start, he tore it down to the frame and cleaned its every moving part. If the VW Bug swapped from a buddy didn't idle, he rebuilt the carburetor. If the Chevy truck didn't shift right, he jacked it up and tore the transmission apart. I don't think he ever went to a gas station for repairs. None of this was remarkable except he laid below the engines in any weather. Howling wind and snow couldn't keep him from the pavement, or the most vexing mechanical problems. I saw his feet protrude from the undercarriage on my way to the post office, wedged between grease and a possible gift to his family, a car or motorcycle that ran. I respected his tenacity when the booze wasn't speaking for him.

His younger son showed up one day, the first I'd seen of him. We talked when I passed and he worked around the house for weeks. Then a neighbor alluded to something more—how I should be aware of him—the law might be close behind. I didn't care for rumor; it was the candy of quick judgment to adduce the greater suspicion: he was out of work because of his past. I understood this, having volunteered at the prison for years. The indiscretion that brought us together was harmless—he would earn my respect or not.

*   *   *

In the middle of Jake leaving, Debby lost her father. Losing him complicated the tumult down the street. Bob was a man for whom living in one place, working in a 9-to-5 job, was tantamount to a slow death. As a teenager he worked endlessly to support his family and enlisted as a pilot in World War II. Twice he was shot down and parachuted behind enemy lines. That's where he met Gladys, Debby's mom. She was in the Belgian underground as a teenager and together with her villagers, rescued the allied pilots and kept the orphaned Jews in their houses. They were heroes before I was old enough to vote. I was the last one to join the family. By then Bob had to resign from the corporate accounting world to keep Gladys from living in the humid Florida heat. They returned to California and it was never easy for him after that. Bad deals, borrowed money, and the swagger to defend them came falling down on their family.

I was thinking about him driving home from Hawthorne, thinking how much he loved what I saw: sixteen big horn sheep with two newborns scampering up the rock for mother's milk. In the Mason Valley estuary, there were dozens of migrating ibises. A red-tail sat on a nest in the cottonwood. They were gifts I had not expected those few days before Easter when to pray seemed an only choice: Bob died a week ago. Like Jake, he stood on the street when he visited, smoking, looking for birds, for signs of life in the burnished land. We spent a week in the hospital, the Adventist caregivers were like angels in that time of hurried doctoring. All we could ask them was would he live? In the seesaw of seven days he answered us. He answered with everything in his being and then he left, just as Debby and I and her brother and his wife left the California vineyard where he now rests. After the stroke, he made it to his eighties, falling on the stairwell of a VA bus.

The ghost of his hobbled frame haunts us now. He came to this place frequently but the high altitude drew him down. Some nights he coughed until we thought he would aspirate and suddenly die. But always, when the sun rose, it was "Hi, guy," like he meant it, followed by a smoke, a shave, and the news. He ate oatmeal, drank coffee with milk and one sugar, and admonished me to fill the bird sock. "What are they?" he asked each day of his visit.

"Goldfinches, like the ones at your house."

"Oh..." he sighed like a child. What drew him to birds and flowers I could only guess and then pretend to notice with him, for the first time, how each small petal of color or red or yellow breast returned. That was almost enough for nearly a decade until he couldn't live with the idea of doing more in his tangled body. We tried to comfort him with the natural beauty out the window. In all of his stupored grace, he gave us his attention to the wild. I think he wanted to fly his whole life and the pilot of his early years was an approximation, grafted from his dreams. He was never happy in the kind of carnival 9-5 existence that takes so much from our days. He wanted to be above what we could experience here on land. I respect him for that, even if it tore at the tissue of those he loved, my wife among them. His love letters written after the war were imprimaturs of something larger than a man and his bride beholden to the limits of his job and house. They were testimony to what the novelist bares in the pages of a story: the kinetic truth of staying alive, and what the poet yearns to unearth in line after line: something like ecstasy. It's not hard to understand his sorrow: it is the sorrow of a man who wanted more than his flesh would permit. That never translated well to a life of routines but it made him the permanent fixture of pub, café, and conversation. He could talk on any subject, however exaggerated, and frequently with a joy that let him rise above the commonplace and then, magically, he was back, time after time, to the man he once was to startle with a fresh observation of what had flown or grown in the time he was away.

Of all those requisite regrets that visit a man, these failings of family he knew well. What came easiest to him—being a former provider, a former war hero—was lost when he returned home. There was no stage to perform on; only the hush of family.

*   *   *

Jake walked out the door, rake in hand, wanting to talk. I recoiled, never sure of what was about to happen. His second son had written from prison. He was in love. He wanted to spend the rest of his days with a woman he met through the mail—not the white gang he had sworn to uphold, the one that kept him alive in the joint. His only way out of it was death or disappearance.

I nodded, as if to acknowledge the ancient bargain his son had struck with this woman. Yes, I knew a love worth keeping. What could he do? Jake asked me, like I was entrusted with a subtle knowledge, an unnatural deference in the small bead of daylight. "They'll hurt her, they'll end it before he gets out," he coughed in the locust trees. I didn't have an answer, and I didn't like that this threat lurked before the one good thing his son found in prison, someone to love. We waited out the silence, the uneasy wind until he said, "Well, maybe it'll work out."

"Maybe," I confided.

He leaned on the rake for minutes, tried to find words to break the tension. What is it a man does with this contorted version of his son falling in love? He shares it on a street in the mountains. He hopes it will find purchase in a man beyond the fences. He imagines a feral conclusion and then retires to his rake. I could summon no courage and walked home. I had nothing for Jake. I could not tell my family. It would only haunt them. Besides, it's become clear that in the breath of this man, something wants out that will not be described save by paradox, and the two of us will do our best with what we cannot say.

*   *   *

We live in a small town. Bob was loved by all of our friends and that love came around the corner to pay its due: cards and flowers arrived. Friends told us they had read the obituary, they did not know how they could help but they wanted to. The kitchen table filled with flowers from people who knew Debby's father in ways that only they could—the jocular man who smoked in any weather and hailed the bulbs and finches weeks ago. He had a secular wisdom that was lost on his family, a family that was bruised from living downwind of his dreams.

＊　　　　　　＊　　　　　　＊

The trucks showed up at Jake's house today. Men with tattoos and white pants are gutting it. The piles of wood grow outside the front window. I ask them, "Is it ruined?"

"Nah," they shake their heads. Still it will be weeks before it is ready to inhabit. I want to go inside, to see what it took to stay alive in there. One night when the former tenants lived there, we sat at their kitchen table. They, too, had a rough ride of joblessness and angry teenagers. I began to think the persistence of hunger was in the walls. I remember that night: the man fired one-liners at his son, his boozy breath close behind. His wife stared at me like I would never understand. She was right, almost. I couldn't say anything to assuage them and scuttled to the door. Maybe the house was coming down in effigy. Maybe this was a final gasp of someone who tried to make what they could in the world and then borrowed another twenty and drove on. Maybe this was the parish of failed wishes camped on the lawn with a busted Chevy truck. Maybe this was the altar of what could have been.

Maybe this was all Jake could bare when he showed up at my house one Saturday morning. "What time's the Boar's Head Feast?"

Debby and I looked at each other like the moon had slipped from its rails—"*What?*" we asked in unison.

"That art dinner. That tonight?"

"Yes... I think so. Call Piper's—I'm sure they know." The Celtic Festival was held at the opera house every winter. But I never expected Jake to go. He was wheezing, bad, looked like he was starved for air, for what to say.

"You want to come in?"

"I can't stay."

His speech was truncated, never certain of tomorrow, and then it burst like a bubble: "I just want to tell you. You guys were the good ones; I was the asshole. I got emphysema, docs don't know what else and they put me on something to calm me, I can't remember, but it's just shit, you know, this goddamn thing's gonna kill me, anyway I just wanted you to know how good you were to me and my family. I'm sorry I fucked it all up. That day you picked my wife up from the ice and it was just near dark, I don't know what-all she'd a done if you hadn't. My kids, what they been through, all that, I don't have words really, I just come to tell you."

Then he left in the snow on Saturday morning. Debby and I looked at each other, at Jake's footprints in the path to the gate. Neighbors. This is the land of living with and for someone. It is as hard as anything I have ever done. No doubt Jake would say the same. It didn't make it any easier to relinquish the rubble outside his window, nor his grandkids that floated in from Reno like kites. They were in bad marriages, bad hotels, and sometimes before he snapped, there was a little peace when a great-grandkid sat on Jake's lap. "Yep, she's down with Stinkass. I told him if he ever lays a hand on her again… but what the hell, she'll go back—"

In high school, the oldest granddaughter wanted to be a hairdresser. She took classes in a program to accelerate her progress. When she walked to school she was attractive and happy—on most days. There was a boyfriend in a car with tinted windows. They almost seemed innocent together. At graduation Jake and I nodded at one another, our exchange student was her friend. How ironic, these two people colliding in a small town. A year and a half later she was home with her baby-to-be, and then she was gone. In and out until the cycle broke and Jake told me it was over. No more. No more coming home. She wasn't gonna listen, "but who did?" he sighed. "Who did?"

*　　　　*　　　　*

In a few days we'll go to the service for my father-in-law. He will be laid to rest in a veteran's cemetery. He will be proud and released from this place that never understood what it was he wanted. He will live in the nexus of his two lands, the hoped for and the forgotten. He will be eulogized at a beautiful altar with other veterans and we will patch together the quandary of his life.

When I was young I made a prayer: at thirty my boys will not be trying to reconcile their relationship with me. It was to myself, naturally, because raising children is both sacred and terrifying. They must never know you care for them more than yourself, and yet they know it every day. Fathers leave their traces. Jake left his. I wonder which car he is driving now, which two-lane is widening into the future? What girls sit in the back with their father, grandfather, or great-grandfather? What country are they swerving into, what brilliant expanse lies ahead? Thank God for the open highway. It has left Jake room in the West. But it is not a place to which he can return. It is simply a place of memory. Tomorrow I could get a call from him, lost in a downtown café, and it could all start again.

Every day when I leave for work, the men in the white pants toss more from the house. It is like a bare face now. Toys, couches, and barbeques are splayed on the dry grass. It is early May and a few bulbs flail in the decay. Something will return a man to this place, a person who comes here to remake his life, stake his best chance on the edge of this mountain. Someone will wake and methodically go to work, return to the kitchen, the food, and the faces sitting there and I will know they have arrived when the torment squeaks from the door—unless, of course, there is peace inside. The first family who lived there was the most gracious we have known. They were horse breeders with children who could not lie. This is when the house seemed idyllic and the paintings I did of it were not so dark. This is when it was an address of refuge, a place you could return to for safety, a place that reached across fences and into the fabric of neighbors.

The workers continue, the dust flies east. Yesterday the owner came to look things over. This was her childhood home, the place she most fondly remembers. When she whispered her name on the porch or out the window, it mysteriously came back. Now she sits on a paint can, peeling an orange with men in white pants. If Jake calls, I will tell him no one is here. There is only dust now, the talisman of what we leave behind.

CHAPTER SIXTEEN

The Bloody Money

This was a week when I needed the light of September. Now midwinter in Virginia City, the snow was dark and there was little to redeem but the cold promise of spring. Even that was not enough to assuage another meeting to find the few dollars needed to push the center forward. An hour and a half later I was on my own: whatever money had once been committed was now gone. It didn't change the need: we still had no place for the before and after-school program which had outgrown its space in the elementary school. We had no place for the at-risk youth education and employment programs, no health clinic, and no meeting place for the other itinerant non-profit programs. In short, we had grown but could not accommodate our need for physical space. Every usable inch in our Victorian office had a desk, a computer, or a file cabinet in it. We kept on working although it was in tight quarters. This only reaffirmed my resolve to get the community center built.

I hadn't heard from Senator Reid's office in some time. When my friend came on the phone, I learned that my contact in Washington was fired—he had lied to many organizations about the funds they were to receive. No wonder it had taken five years: nothing was being done. My friend told his replacement, "Whatever you do, don't lie to him." Fair enough, welcome to DC politics: for a lobby-less non-profit on the edge of a mountain in the Great Basin, we had been elevated to a first-name basis with the new staff member, who assured me his word was good. Eighteen months later we received our first federal appropriation for the center in 2004: $347,935. I was out of the country when Senator Reid presented the check, but gratefully our staff was present for the photo. It was the first tangible indication of the center. I was still 2.7 million dollars short, but it gave the project credence; it set our organization on a path to becoming a visible presence in the community.

In order to access those funds, we had to do multiple studies to determine the site was non-toxic and was not a sinkhole to one of the hundreds of shafts below ground. We had signed a thirty-year lease with the county to build the center on the tennis courts—which of course, by the time we received that first appropriation—had a divot the size of a Fiat on one of the courts. But after many years of dialogue, the site was thought to be best for the community: close to other county facilities like the park, the pool, and senior center.

This and other costs I could not foresee (historic, geologic, and archeological surveys, etc.) whittled that initial sum considerably. But for the first time we could pay Art, our architect, and his plans were soon forthcoming. Quickly we realized that enclosing the pool was folly: another million and year-round heating and circulation costs. Given our low-budget operation, development of a scale that would be required to raise two million was quite enough. Back to the architect—make the building smaller and keep the core facilities intact.

Twice we went back to Senator Reid for funds: Hurricane Katrina and the war in Iraq scuttled those requests. In the interim, I began the journey into private fund-raising—small foundation grants to keep the project moving forward. A local bank gave us $30,000 for architectural fees and we held numerous dinners, special events and ceremonies to mark the occasion of the center's hoped-for birth: a symbolic ground-breaking when we had little more than a shovel to show for our progress. We raised a sign on the future site but had to repaint the start date with every year that went by. Then the sign was stolen. Perhaps the vandals needed it more than us. Perhaps there had been recognition of its potential on this site.

We installed a skate park on the tennis court without the sinkhole. At last there was something for young people to do in their free time: bike and skate and rollerblade up and down the ramps and bars. This, at least, is what we had hoped for: an opportunity to build cohesion among young people, to develop in them a sense of service and pride. This was their facility. They needed to take care of it, and needed just as badly, to use it.

Vandals struck again and quickly made the place a liability. Somehow the progress we had envisioned was coming to a slow and virtual halt. It seemed that each step forward was an unfilled promise and soon people began to question our credibility: what was it we were doing and why? Why not just leave things alone? Clearly, no one wanted the negative consequences that came with such a skate park, no one except those we served. Youth rarely have a voice in the decisions that affect them. But they liked the skate park and they used it so we repeatedly tried to find a way to make that possible. I am reminded of the bean field in John Nichols' novel, *The Milagro Beanfield War*: the park became a symbol of defiance and we inherited the role of its defender.

Neither of these were choices we wanted. In fact, they were the antithesis of what was hoped for: a place for youth to gather where there had been none. But such is the work of dreams: if it were just a bean field or skate park it would have been benign but it was not. It was, instead, a place of play and conflict—something that was never intended. And dreams often end before they are fulfilled.

*   *   *

Yesterday, a reporter called to pit me between the governor and his wife over the latest cuts to the biennial budget. How does this happen? One day you're sitting at a desk trying to maneuver between Faustian budget cuts and the next, you suddenly are a spokesman for what people are thinking. I declined any knowledge of intent and resented the inference that I should make such a choice.

A friend called at the end of the day to ask for help: she had inadvertently upset a colleague while trying to get support for a bill to improve the lives of kids. This is the detritus of our work—grief for doing what is needed or right. After a long conversation I wrote her these words: 'Try to remember these are the consequences of change, of pushing people to move forward, even inches, and in the chaos of this work, come the unintended sparks of indignation. The kids are what matters, they are at the helm of this work, not those who profess to lead. Know that their voices that are rejoicing, especially when the sparks arise because they have at last, been heard.'

*   *   *

It is a whiteout beyond the window. I shoveled the propane tank, the driveway, and the woodpile, but it has all returned. An Alaskan cold front. The office is closed. Our most hardy employees drove up Geiger Grade from Reno but the plows cannot keep up and they returned home. A day for reflection and wood fire. Heat in the igloo that is my home.

I kept trying to raise enough private revenue to start the center. It scared me: to ask for $15,000 was one thing; for ten times that amount was quite another. I imagined that if four foundations became partners we could finish the first phase of the project. I wrote them with my idea. By then we had received one more federal grant with Senator Reid's help and several small foundation contributions. We were still a long way from digging, from doing anything more than talking or planning and consequently, it was just an idea. To get a foundation to step forward and make a major contribution—without any concrete certainty that the idea would come to fruition—was almost laughable.

One of the foundation directors called and asked to meet. For one hour, I was grilled on every possible nuance of the building: its design, access, and structure, its fiscal, political, and legal governance, its land and ownership liability, its long-term operations, its integration into the future of Storey County and Community Chest, its construction timetable given the risk of an unfinished structure and lastly, my ability to raise two million dollars. Our deputy director, Erik Schoen, sat through the meeting—one of the most vulnerable sixty minutes either of us can recall. Afterwards he confided: "I had no idea what was involved."

Nor had I until I began my research into building such a facility. Even then I was woefully out of place when I met with the architects and engineers. We hired a consultant to tell us what every step would cost. It was like a foreign language but I had no choice: learn it or lose this opportunity. I studied things far from any of my books in college: bidding, contracts, insurance, the merits of wood versus metal construction, and site preparation at the hoped-for multi-use facility. I remember the engineer telling the architect, "It will never happen." Perhaps he articulated what the others had long felt—this was a dream and nothing more. Then I thought what gives him the right? He's just getting paid; we are doing this because we must.

In about two months I received a letter from the foundation director: if you raise $150,000 we will match it. A second foundation wrote with a similar proposition: if you raise $50,000 we will match it. The other two foundations did not respond. This was a mixed blessing: I was thrilled that they had both made a commitment but I did not have any notion of where to turn for the matching contributions. A total of $200,000 on paper with a promise of its release once I found $200,000 more.

More research. I wrote every major donor within a hundred miles and convened a board to help me with this process. All of them had development experience. I gave them boilerplate proposals but nothing came of it. Then a friend called to ask if I would work with her on a proposal to bring health care to Storey County. "Of course," I said. Nearly a year passed and no word. Then, almost overnight, it was funded. This was the lynchpin I thought. This would anchor the center. If there was funding for the health care facility, this would offset the revenue loss for the rest of the first phase.

There were still no matching funds. I kept writing and thinking, even returned to an old nemesis—a very large foundation that had initially encouraged us. The staff and board grew weary of living in the future tense, the tense of tomorrow, of *if* but they were patient, true believers in the best sense of Eric Hoffer's ideal. I continued to send proposals to Senator Reid each winter but could not foresee what political events would arise to delay the funds. A war, a hurricane, a loss of one political party and this smallest of Congressional requests, $200,000, vanished like a gust of wind.

In the fall the staff and board come together for an annual retreat. Out of that process emanates our goals for the year, an affirmation of who we are and what we need to do given the ever-changing landscape of this work. Whether it's domestic violence or jobs, veterans or food, the only constant is the refrain: get it done. At the next board meeting I asked what the group most wanted from this year. All of them looked at me and said, "Build the center." I swallowed and asked again. "Build the center."

*　　　　　　*　　　　　　*

Another day of harrowing testimony at the legislature: parents of children with autism trying to find their way forward with little hope of programs or support. My fearless colleague, Christy McGill, sent a text message: God, this is terrible. Two stories below them I was in a room with the artists, librarians, and museum directors— all of us stuck on a pin of little recourse. When I returned to the office, I spoke to Erik: we have become trivial, our voices are like flies drumming against the glass. He was haunted and frustrated. There seemed no discernable way forward and still the courage to find new revenue limped from the room.

The wind scored the streets and the trees; dust was everywhere, the constant, and the harbinger of toil in the high desert. Snow would have been a relief. Dust is dry and granular—it needs no home—a metaphor for the transience that pervades this state. To be rootless is not an aspiration, it is not something to need or want. Still, whether it is gaming or the boom and bust cycles of mining, this place attracts and disperses people like so many leaves. Yet, for the dozens of families at the legislative dais, there can be no other place to live. They have children with special needs; they are not emissaries to another locale. This is always the difficulty—translating what Nevada means to an outsider. It is a hardscrabble landscape, an unforgiving place and to many, unattractive. But there is no definition of its endless quiet, its variegated, sculpted mountains and basins, its sky and light. Rootlessness has ravaged this place, our culture come and gone for a hundred and fifty years. Twain knew it in the 1860s and we know it now. This is our dark side, our sense of temporary existence in this landscape. To talk about the importance of the arts, the humanities, of libraries God forbid, is to be suspect, to be misinformed and clearly out of place with this land. That is why, sitting before the legislators, I never feel comfortable: most believe we are more than the sum of our past. They expect its poets, writers, painters, musicians, and dancers to put their legacy in the context of something greater, a uniform belief in the value of cultural and artistic life. This rarely happens. The very qualities that are the bulwark against the repeated boom and bust cycles of this state—books, music, museums, art, an educated workforce—are the first to be excused from the room when they collide with money and expediency.

It doesn't matter that words are not heard now—we must speak until they are. This is not futility, rather a presumed desire to take back the land and its people, to reaffirm what is noble and distinct, our patrimony that cannot be replicated. This is the West, damned and desired, drenched with light and story, Paleolithic and present, the edge of millennia right outside the door. This is worth redeeming, worth reclamation in the most hopeful sense: we reclaim what we love. The rest goes by unnoticed, untamed.

A West unknown. Perhaps that is the West we want to inhabit: the one that exists in the imagination, the one that can never be had. Surely our ancestors would drum for a chance at such a land. Even the Basque shepherds wandered in search of this very isolation: the dream of being alone in paradise far from home. Robert Laxalt's father was a shepherd, his Basque wilderness the Sierra, the alkaline playa, the ridge top of one or two elk, and the drone of wind cuffing the ears. Laxalt, the writerly son, spent a lifetime trying to tame that wilderness. Thankfully, he found fiction to describe it. In so doing, he helped a generation to inhabit this imagined place.

CHAPTER SEVENTEEN

American Flats

It was almost a relief when the squatters set up camp at American Flats. I had driven in to see my friend, Gary Short, who lived in the lone mine shack further down the road. It was midday. The weather was good and there was an old Subaru out front of the metal structure. Two dogs were chained to the front of the building with no heat, water or power. A man and a woman lived there and occasionally there were others. No harm, no foul, I thought. These places, these abandoned mine buildings were scattered throughout the Comstock. Why shouldn't someone live in them? This building sat empty for decades, above a green and oily leach pond. The American Flats stamp mill was built after the heyday of Comstock mining and by the time it was operational, the gold and silver had played out, so it sat vacant after the early 1900s. By now it was scrawled with graffiti and was a hangout for young partygoers on the weekends.

Each time I went out there to see Gary I learned more about the American Flats residents: five-gallon water containers were outside, a barbeque, and a fifty-gallon drum in which to burn the trash. There was a hint of desperation. I wanted to ask what brought them to this place, this unlikely refuge that had been condemned to silence for decades. I wanted to know what peculiar circumstance rose at their heels to chase them from their last home. I wanted to know how someone lives on a concrete floor through the winter. The road into American Flats becomes a mud hole once the snow flies. Even the propane truck gets stuck en route to Gary's house. This condition would only leave them more isolated in the empty buildings.

The irony was that the mining property was little more than a tax write-off for the shell companies who came and went. What did their stockholders know of the drop in property values or the tenants who had settled in the remnants of this place? Gary paid rent to the unscrupulous front man for these companies. It became hard to take anything he said seriously.

The squatters remained and the camp outside their door took on an orderly appearance. Driving in, I waved at the man in the doorway. He looked happy, as if that simple act was an affirmation of his presence in this forlorn place. The dogs barked, I was still a stranger. I wanted to stop and talk but was weary of what I could not see. In that ongoing dilemma of little guy versus big, I rooted for them each time I drove by until finally he walked from the door to greet me. He asked me in. I declined, but we talked for some time. He had nothing to hide but he had no shelter. He was one of many who lived on deserted land in this vast, open wilderness. I asked if the cops had been out and he shook his head, no, the message being, don't say a thing. "Not a word," I said and drove on to see Gary.

Gary is a poet and he lives in the mine shack between teaching gigs, workshops, and almost any other work he can muster. He writes poems on the porch of the former mine office. He looks out on the green lake below and sometimes there is a seagull circling overhead. Occasionally I bring Nevada and he hits golf balls from the fake grass mat with Gary. He calls it his private putting green.

This place is open, set on a large stretch of level ground. There are three homes further up the canyon and they have a spring. One of the owners made a pond for the trout that somehow survive the coyotes and the ice of winter. The homeowners, too, drive by the squatters every day. They go to work, pick their kids up from the bus stop and return to this canyon. I have thought of living up the canyon where they have their houses. It is barely ten miles from the state capital but it is the most hidden place on the Comstock. Perhaps that's what drew the squatters here. It is certainly what drew the sheepherder who comes each June with his flock and his busted-up trailer, a fifty-gallon water drum outside. Strangely, I felt more at ease talking to him, a Peruvian here on an extended visa. He worked for almost no wage, but enough to send something home to his wife and child in Lima. When a rattler came to his trailer he killed it with a rock, thrown straight at its head. He has a gun for the coyotes that nightly come for the weakest in his flock.

Where do the squatters go when someone comes for them? They run, I guess, run to the next place where there are fewer people, fewer eyes to notice them. They have perfected the art of living invisibly, living without a trace of their existence. They have no prior life, they are stranded in the present, the day-to-day of staying alive. They are not unlike the thousands without shelter in this state—an anomaly shared only by those who experience poverty. To most people, the fact of homelessness is not a fact at all; rather, it is an idea that may or may not be true.

The squatters are here for relief from the residue of living without enough money to fully participate in this society. Ironically, the residents of American Flats sought it out for sanctuary. Above the stamp mill is a vast rise west to the Virginia Range, a ridge of piñon and juniper. There are cottonwoods that follow the spring to the level ground and some days when I visit Gary, a red-tailed hawk circles for the unsuspecting mouse or rabbit. He chose this spot because he could be alone to write and it was one of the few places he could eke out a living.

I must have towed Gary to the highway a dozen times. When the snow comes you can drive it for a few days but when it gets warm it turns to mud. His old car makes it to the first hill and sometimes to the second, but then, invariably, I get a call. My Jeep is thin on style but I yank him from the ditch without going into four-low. I follow him to the highway and wish sometimes I were free like him, to pursue my art any hour of the day. Over the years, he has shared the opposite thing: he wishes he had a family and did not have to be nomadic to stay alive. The one thing he wanted more than anything was permanency.

Gary tells more about the squatters. The man has found a job in town. He hopes to make enough money to get into an apartment. He asked Gary if he would take his dogs, but of course he cannot, given his own itinerant life. Gary must follow what little money there is in poetry.

The squatters make it through one winter before they find a place to live in town. The woman he is with waits tables at a restaurant. They are able to bathe regularly, wash clothes, and cook, little things that most of us don't think about. The man joins on with a construction crew. He's a hard worker, and develops the respect of the others who work outside in any weather. I see him in his old Subaru, he waves at me every time and every time I promise to keep my secret.

Later, the woman comes to our office. I do not ask what brings her here. Confidentiality is everything in a small town. I can see that she is uncomfortable. I leave her with colleagues with whom she can be anonymous.

*   *   *

Not a day goes by without someone like her coming into our office. I don't have to ask where they live; their address is unknown. It is a field, a hill, a ravine, a spot to lie down, shelter in its most basic form. For years there was a mentally ill man, benign to most who lived here, who called another mine shack home. No one asked why he had to live there but many helped him. Again, because there was room for tolerance, he lived in that shack for more than a decade. He had a bad accident when he was a teenager and this was home, so he stayed. I talked to him on the wooden sidewalks, tried not to avoid him, but it was hard because he could not bathe or change clothes. Sometimes a cigarette would bring a smile to his face or a tourist would hand him a twenty. Embarrassed, he stuffed it in his pocket and walked to the next container looking for food.

A woman came to our office in the middle of winter, needing a ride home—four miles into the mountains. The road was almost impassable, two feet of snow and a river below when it crossed the ravine. She has lived without amenities for years. She muddles by on social security. She, too, is mentally ill. Everyone in the office has worked with her, has driven her and her minimal belongings to a room. Everyone has learned to tolerate the dog that can sleep in any quarters. But almost as certainly, she returns with anger and that is the last time we see her. One woman walked for three days from Reno to Virginia City to get services in our office. She had no real problems; she just needed a job. She was in her fifties, over the hill for a cook. No family nearby and nothing to rely on. When she left our office she told me it was the first time someone paid attention to her, someone treated her like a person.

Still another woman with a name that should have woken us up—Person—came in looking for shelter. She, too, grew up in a nearby town and hoped to return to some stasis. Mental illness cut her off from the tendrils of family and so, like the others in the pale light, I drove her to the relative sanctuary of the Reno streets. She refused shelter, refused treatment, but could access food and clothing, harness the smallest of staples for the next day.

*   *   *

The trail up Jumbo Grade parallels the valley of American Flats. I have ridden that trail dozens and dozens of times. At one point the road comes within feet of the water tank for the structures below. From a distance, it appears that the flat is bucolic, the piñon and juniper grow smaller toward McClellan Peak to the south. At the saddle, you can continue west into Washoe Valley and follow the pipeline that brings the Comstock water from Marlette Lake and Hobart Reservoir. In the spring, I measure the moisture we received by the size of the camas lily: occasionally they bloom with a puff of flower and then the wind or the wild horses send them to dust. You can see Reno from that saddle—it is one of the most breathtaking views in our region. Mt. Rose is due west and Washoe Lake is below. To the east, if you turn around, is the Great Basin, something my eyes have never tired of seeing. In the fall, when you move south into the canyon below McClellan Peak, you must ride through an aspen grove. There have been times the leaves were so thick I thought it was raining orange and yellow wafers. I braked and waited for them to drop on my head. No one was there. It was shaded with the shadows of a thousand leaves moving to their last winter. Once you ride out of the aspens Carson Valley lies below and Jobs Peak is the next big outline on the southwest horizon. None of this is particularly special to the outsider, but when you walk these places they become more than physical space, they become a place in which to inhabit the mind that brought us here. If you can put aside the notion of any destiny, manifest or otherwise, this place reflects movement of water, rock, tree, and mammal. I reach for that ephemeral mind every time I return to the saddle on Jumbo Grade.

There are countless reminders of our recent past, too—rusted lids, bed springs, bottles, shotgun shells, ceramic beer bottle shards, tin cans, barbed wire and still, every spring, the lupine return. I have tried to transplant them but they refuse the comfort of our yard. They last for about six weeks and then disappear to the rocks and meager soil that keeps them until the following spring. Mule's ears, devil's paintbrush, and cornflowers follow in quick succession. All of them transitory, all of them living in hope of more rain. If it was a good winter, the wildflowers will permeate the ridges above American Flats, and the sheep will graze them flat in a matter of weeks. For an instant, the area becomes something more, something sought after, a place of refuge.

When I ride with Nevada and Cody they try to go up the steep road that heads north from the saddle. Eventually it will come to the back of Mt. Davidson and you can circle to the peak overlooking Virginia City. More than once we have come upon our state bird, the mountain bluebird, which is the color of sidewalk chalk, a pastel blue that is unmistakable from the oily blue of the piñon jays. The kestrel also lives up there and a friend has killed a cougar with a bow on that same ridge. There is abundant wildlife here but we do not always notice. Like the people who choose this valley, they live out of easy sight.

When I was riding south from the saddle to the aspen canyon, something caught the corner of my eye. I slowed and rode back: a rattlesnake had swallowed all but the last of a baby rabbit. I could do nothing but watch in disbelief for twenty minutes. Then, the rattler began to disgorge the rabbit, even though it had probably been two, three weeks without food. I rode on but it was too late to save the rabbit; it was skinned of all hair except what had not been swallowed. Neither snake nor rabbit would be satisfied. When I came back by the rabbit was gone, no doubt a hawk or coyote found him.

It took me a long time to notice such things. I was riding with my eyes closed. When you live here long enough to restore what you lost, in my case attention, you come to understand that American Flats, however disregarded, is a metaphor for the quiet and the calm as much as it is for progress and desolation. It is a metaphor for those of us who live with this contradiction.

CHAPTER EIGHTEEN

Renegades

When Donovan grabbed my hand there was not a bone left unmoved. His fingers were stiff and rough and he held my hand like a hammer. He looked so out of place in the room—a miner from the old school in my office at Community Chest to find out what was wrong. It was 2005. Of course I had the curious distinction among my hard rock friends of being the one who would know such things, but all I really knew was the ground was shifting beneath us. When I met Donovan it was in the Union Brewery, a bar famous for the bras on the roof and the brawls on the floor. His shotgun was pointed at the ceiling and Debby tried to explain that it was probably a good idea to put it down. His son stood next him and pronounced, "That's my dad," but I thought one of us might not make it to the next day. Donovan got about six words out before he fell into me and the barrel bounced off the railing and finally crashed on the floor. There were so many people and the smoke was so thick I doubt anyone saw us on our way down. His son started screaming something about "Don't touch my dad," and I looked at Debby and we hit the door.

It took me years to understand what happened that night: a nocturnal dip in the well spring of Virginia City's run-down saloon, a biker haven that may have been a real watering hole in its heyday but was now a cobweb of women's apparel and a few lost souls on the stools. Donovan didn't shake my hand for another ten years but after that night, he moved closer to what a man might be than almost all the hard rock men I knew. There is a Silver City mill that is his namesake and I think he would still be working it if time and family had not exacted such a cost. His wife had been arrested again, her third DUI, and his son from this marriage was not doing very well. "You gotta fix him, you gotta do that for me. I'm all by myself now…."

Those hands again. Those hands reached for mine. I'd already made up my mind if I ever saw him in a bar I'd call the cops, but now, without the smoke and the crowd, he was literally weeping before me. He released my hand after a minute of shaking. I was grateful nothing felt broken but his girth intimidated my every thought. "Donovan, I can't fix him any more than I can fix the weather but I'll get you some tools to listen, to be his father, to help with school."

"I don't know anything about this stuff but you gotta believe me, I ain't gonna screw this up. He's my son and I love him. And I know you got what he needs."

"No, Donovan. You do. It's going to take time. You can't force this. He's afraid. He doesn't know where his mother is, doesn't know why you pick him up from school. He thinks this is temporary. You have to try to be patient, give him some room to grieve." Donovan looked at me for another minute and I waited for a sign, waited to see who would come back from that worried face.

"What makes you think I can do this? You gonna show me how?"

"I'm going to try but I can't promise she'll change. All I can do is listen, be here with you. Find some resources for your son. You're not alone, Donovan. That's the scary part. We think we're alone and so we make choices that stick with us. I can't outrun what I screwed up and you can't change your wife. You can only be there for your son."

"I wasn't such a good father to my boy, the one you met that night."

"I didn't think you remembered."

"I don't forget those things. I just look like it. He's a good boy, but I can do better. I'm not gonna get this wrong. Don't let me screw it up."

"I won't *let* you do anything. You will. You'll be his father, the man he can trust to never leave. He doesn't know why this is happening. You just have to be with him. If she pulls out of this, he'll see his mother again. If she doesn't, he's got you. That's what you can count on. You and him. Love him when you get up and love him when you go to bed. The rest doesn't matter, Donovan. If you want a son to love, you need to love him every day he's alive. That's what you can do. There will be days when doing that is hard but it can't be any harder than talking to *me*. Hold him, Donovan. He needs you. Don't let him ever doubt it."

Donovan's boots kicked each stair until he turned to say good-bye. I waved but could be not certain of any comfort given. In the most unholy time of this trade, that moment when a person reveals what little self remains, there is never enough language to console. The theoreticians who came before us have stamped this profession with cures, but I think the cure is not far from the hands. I don't mean to trivialize all of the good that comes from the practice of counseling. It is certainly one of the profound discoveries of our time: the weaving of solace into a life. Surely it has happened for thousands of years before we understood its power, but we do now, and Donovan was loath to conceal his expectations. I was not. My friends in this town have shaken with pain, but when a miner comes for something that cannot be given, it is a pain altogether different, a pain without a healer for the quick, permanent cure. I suppose, if I went to him for his expertise and he said, "No, I can't assay this sample, but you can," I'd feel cheated by language and leave in a huff. Maybe that's what he wanted to do but he didn't. I learned to measure his grief with each handshake that followed.

His bum leg bounced to the chair and then he turned to report: "The court says it will be six more months. She's sober and has been calling my son. We went to see her last weekend. She might pull out of this, Shaun. She just might."

"How's your son? How's he doing in school? What about his friend? Did he move away?"

"Teacher said he's reading almost to his grade. I thought they were gonna hold him back but hey, maybe not. It's a damn miracle I ain't coughed up dead from all this. You know what I'm saying?

Them reports about his mother being gone. I'm doing the dishes, fixing something to eat for him."

"No one's after you, Donovan. No one's gonna' take your son."

Donovan came to the office to share every step his son took, and when his mother got out of jail, he thought it was over, the rush to love for both parents with one unified set of hands. I was cautious but hoped it might be over too. She came home for a while, started drinking, and he finally kicked her out. She left for another state, Texas I think, and then my friend died, too old for the spirit of a young boy. The court gave her custody and in the malaise of a broken system, it might be better than foster care. It might also ruin him. Donovan gave me reason to pause every time I saw him. As stern a man as any gun could mask, and then some other man rose to meet me in the quiet of an office.

*　　　　　　*　　　　　　*

Louie came down Washington in his old Chevy, the alligator headdress with a mannequin leg sticking out of its mouth over the cab. Louie was never quite complete without the coonskin cap dangling from his brow. He stopped to pick up the carcass of a magpie—hard as it was to imagine—and laid it on a retired telephone cable spool in his front yard. His wife of some years, Carolyn, came outside to unearthly calm. What she witnessed she never tired of telling. We were meeting at the library, ten of us gathered to discuss poetry. Carolyn, Louie's counterpart in charismatic storytelling, began slowly. "One by one they came out of the locust trees and stood on the telephone spool for more than a minute, then returned to the trees. More than twenty birds. For over an hour they paid tribute to their kin on that spool. And not a sound in the air."

"A magpie funeral?" we asked, almost in unison. I had never heard of such a thing but knowing Louie, could only further speculate on the gravity of the procession. "In your front yard?" I questioned, incredulous that birds could have such holy moments of parting.

Louie drove a truck for forty years and often as not brought it down Washington Street, parked it outside his house that was part fort and part counterculture way station. The Indian totem pole welcomed all comers to the pine plank exterior, skinned from logs he hauled. It was closer in design to Neruda's boathouse in Isla

Negra than any historically themed structure in Virginia City. Room attached to room in no particular order, but he never sacrificed the view. The living room glass faced east, beneath the cover of locust, pine, and a field of myrtle below. There were outbuildings and stacks of every kind of lumber known to carpenter and Louie alike. If he could gather it, it was in his yard: tires, benches, cables, spools, trucks from at least three decades, and of course, the inimitable poodle that rode shotgun with Louie on every trip.

On most days, Louie left for work before dawn and at day's end, he stretched to a long shadow in the Washoe Club, his stool a preacher's distance from the lingering bar flies. Louie started in and sometimes rolled to a cinematic finish before pointing the Chevy to home, which miraculously, found its way to the edge of the drive. Carolyn cajoled the wild man that came in the door. Louie brought home animals, dead and alive, one, two, and four legs, and frequent visitors to the high church of Washington whose colossus alternately provided shelter, reprieve, or hideout from a badge in a neighboring county. In a small town, some people have access to privilege of position, regardless of their circumstance or station. Louie was as much at home at Lynn Leong's Sharon House restaurant as Gordon Lane's Union Brewery. The high brow, the low brow, the small, and the diffident—it made no difference to Louie. He never chose to understand the word *anger*. He was here for one reason: to live every day, work just enough to put some food on the table and keep the pub tab open. He was fortunate, too, to run afoul of the law no more than once, when they brought him home and remanded him to Carolyn's custody. The law was partial to Louie as caretaker of the rich cultural tradition of drinking on the Comstock. As long as he held sway from his stool, no one thought the wiser.

Justice looked the other way for the longest time in Storey County. To the outsider, it made no sense: the cathouses were ten minutes from the state capital in neighboring Lyon County, but they were illegal where the state's business was done. Prostitution was likewise tolerated in Storey County, as evidenced by the queen of judicial affairs high atop the courthouse: one eye has been closed to unsightly habits for most of the last century. A cathouse in other communities is a lecherous wound. In this small county it's an institution. The greatest irony is what happens to those in its service. The sheriff was perfectly selected for office in successive elections, the girls having been polled on the virtues of the democratic process. And the commissioners, similarly emboldened, let well enough alone so long as they could be the leaders of regard. This led to something that even the renegades couldn't fathom: permission to misbehave as long as no one got hurt.

A further irony was not lost on Debby and me when we came before the commissioners for initial approval of the preschool, and later, minimal funding for youth programs. It was Conforte's former madam who understood what we were saying. She became our biggest proponent—the lone female commissioner in Storey County.

This permission must have had an impact on the district attorney's inclination to forgive. One morning, Debby and I were walking to breakfast at the Palace when his excellence, after a particularly long night of imbibing, gave her the gooiest kiss she may have ever received from someone twice her age. He, needless to say, had no memory of the event in the ensuing daylight, which like the occasional memory loss, served the county well. The prosecution rests your honor, as it did in most things civil, criminal, and beyond. Storey County had no literal legal boundaries save the most heinous of crimes… like insinuating an elected official might be on the take, but in its jaded, imperfect way, it worked. Worked like justice works on most of the globe—we take care of our own and you best not bother with whatever it is you aim to change. Fair enough. Rules were rules. Which is why Louie gave the greatest of pleasure—he broke them for sport and still managed an entire adult life without apology or excuse. There was a bit of the outlaw in Louie, and county elders couldn't be bothered with his shenanigans. Nothing of their affairs was ever documented but the rumors kept things in perfect balance: as long as Conforte dealt the cards, business proceeded just fine. About the time Louie got the sugar and went into a wheelchair, Conforte left for Brazil. This did prove to be a real downfall for many—our longest serving female commissioner went to jail, the sheriff ran out of excuses, the DA fell to lesser things, and the lone living commissioner suspected of being on Conforte's payroll died just before he was to go to trial. Sometimes I joke with Debby that had we wanted to open a cathouse, it might have been easier, which may be why Louie thrived in our small town and why so many were drawn to its abandoned frontier.

Louie's mother-in-law was a wood sculptor. In the back of her house stood life size pieces—birds, busts, bears, mothers, and daughters. Nothing about this was remarkable except Marjorie was just over five feet and had hewn the logs with a chainsaw. Self-taught, she whittled them with a chisel and hammer until the wood rose to reveal its most personal quality. There were dozens of these pieces, some in Louie's home, in the galleries of Reno and Carson and still she thought of herself as a woman who worked in wood. The relative peace they brought to her life was palpable. Louie respected her art and paradoxically, Carolyn's interest in poetry. How is it a man bound to an eighteen-wheeler can slide from a bar stool to an art gallery? Louie never thought to ask and Carolyn let well enough alone. Perhaps that's why it worked. She could do worse than an alligator headdress on his flatbed cab. Throughout his tempestuous comings and goings, something else gave way—their daughter found her way to the Comstock. She began catering meals and ran more than one restaurant while raising her own brood, her feckless husband hushed in the distance. In her I saw a wellspring of kindness rise from Louie and Carolyn like a vase of cornflowers, an indigenous gathering of pink, blue, purple, and white blossoms.

In the late spring 2004, Debby and I hosted a group of Zulu singers and dancers. We drove to six northern Nevada cities in nine days and when they came back to Virginia City, Louie's daughter asked them to her house for a meal. By then she was taking care of her grandmother, the wood sculptor who was nearly one hundred, and when the young performers walked in, she looked up and said, "Honey, there's a black man in the house." Louie's daughter laughed like her late father and then realized her grandmother, the artist, spoke with the innocence of a child when they arrived. When they started to sing, her grandmother joined them and before long was nearly swept from her chair in their arms, so spiritual was their sound.

*   *   *

Butch yanked the car door open—"You're a shrink, you know what to do," the inference being you drive a car, you know why it starts. "I'm desperate, I don't know what to do. I've given him money, sent him to school, and he just can't get a job. Is there something wrong with him? You gotta' tell me *now.*"

Butch sat in my cab for forty-five minutes on Virginia City's main street before I drove on. None of this would have mattered but Butch was part of my life, and of almost every resident of the Comstock who had a roof. Whatever the problem, he came to fix it, a cigarette butt hanging from his lip and a stray in his pickup. Gruff, ornery, and he could cuss the frock off a nun, but not a winter went by without a call: "Shaun, I'm gonna send you $100 for the Community Chest. You use it on food. I don't want it leaving this county. You know who needs it."

I met Butch working on the preschool. Like all of the parents, he donated his time, and the building wouldn't pass code without him. We renovated a residential home and he came every Saturday for months, stripped the shingles off, replaced the plywood, unrolled the tarpaper, and put new composition shingles in their place. A roofer must work in any weather and Butch had his share. When the raindrops literally fell to my desk, he told me "There's nothing left up there. I can patch it but it will be leaking before the winter's out."

After his wife left him and took her exotic fish, he was lost and this contributed to his sense of urgency. "I can't figure it out. When he got out of high school, he wanted to fix jet engines so I sent him to this airplane tech school. More money than I make in a year. They said they'd place him. What the hell's wrong, Shaun? Why can't a kid get a job today? I'd put him to work but he doesn't want anything to do with this goddamned trade. I feel like he's fucked and he's not even twenty-one. What am I gonna do?"

"There's nothing to *do,* Butch, but be there for him—"

"What the fuck's that mean? I can fix any roof on this mountain but I don't know a thing about *being* there for him. What kind of faggot-shit you saying anyway?"

Butch didn't understand any man whose trade took him into an office. Then came the trump card: "What would you do—if it were your boy?" like my boys were in the chorus at Julliard.

"Tell him you love him, Butch. Tell him to go on a date. Tell him to keep looking for work."

Butch rubbed his head and blew the cigarette smoke in my face. His teeth were stained from chew. How any woman could love him was beyond me. But they did, some better than others. Sheila was ten years his junior and tried in her earnest way to make Butch happy. Which meant dressing in coveralls and kneepads, and scaling a ladder to pitch roofing supplies to her old man. She could handle a nail gun and light a smoke in a hard wind. From the back, she was all woman, but her face was hardened with living. Walking out to my car, he drove by, backed up and hollered, "You got any ideas what's wrong with *her*?"

"Who, Butch?"

"Sheila—"

"Sheila who?"

"You know. That skirt I been seeing. She left, says it's the booze, but I don't know. What the fuck's that got to do with anything? I give her a bed, feed her well, even cleaned out the laundry room so she could find her way. Why can't she just drink at home?"

There were times I had to ask which answer to give, the one before he swung or after? This was one of those times. "Maybe she just needs some space, Butch. Give her time. She'll come around. But even if she doesn't, you've been through this."

"Don't patronize, me you little cocksucker—"

"Butch, if she were here today, would you treat her any different?"

"Than what?"

"Than you treat her now."

"How in the hell do I know?"

"She didn't leave for the booze, Butch."

"Goddamn it, Shaun. Why in the fuck is it so hard?"

"Being with someone?"

"No. Keeping 'em on the couch."

"You want her back?"

"What do you think?"

"Show her, Butch. She doesn't mind going up on the roof with you. She just doesn't like coming down to more of the same."

"Where the fuck do you get that stuff?"

"From people who've been hurt a lot longer than either of us."

"You coming Sunday?"

"To what, Butch?"

"The open house."

"I might."

"I'll buy you a drink for your time. If you can hold your liquor."

He drives away like a gust of wind.

Butch had been working on the hotel roof for two winters. An old building hitched to a new one. Rain and wind and broken shingles kept him employed when almost all of the contractors left the hill. When he did something, he did it right, and if you had to call him back, he never charged. I'm not sure how he stayed in business, because to hear him tell it, he never got paid. "That asshole's into me for two grand in materials and now he's asking for more work?"

"Maybe you ought to stop."

"Well, you know how he is—"

"Just because he can hurt you doesn't mean you have to give him what he wants."

"I'm not gonna *give* him a goddamned thing if he doesn't pay me."

"This isn't about the money."

"I need the money."

"Not his money. Let the snow do its work. When he's tired of it, he'll pay you." He lit the butt, looked down the canyon, put his hand on my shoulder, and said, "You talkers are all alike. You can't do a fucking thing but you can borrow your way out of it."

"That's why I like you, Butch. You're so quick to compliment—"

"I wasn't talking about you, asshole." More smoke and he rolls down the road.

CHAPTER NINETEEN

When the Ones You Love Go Down

It had been ten years since Debby I and flew to Manhattan Beach, California, to bring in the New Year with Jun, Jess's uncle, in 1991. All of Jess's family was gathered for a huge spread of sushi, rice, and vegetables. It was foggy by the beach. We stood at the perimeter of the table and tried to find things to say. The one person I wanted to see was no longer in the room.

I would have this feeling of emptiness for years. It would presage much of what followed. Jess died the year we started Community Chest. I would often reflect on his experience in the northern California mountains, trying to start a school without enough resources. I spoke to him as if he were still alive—what would you do in this situation? How would you handle the vagaries of payroll, building an office, hiring staff for needs that were yet to be funded? I never imagined he had the answers; I knew him too well for that. But it was his willingness to listen to what we were getting into that I relied on. And so I did. I talked to him in every weather, like he was present for the decisions that nearly crippled us—when the commissioners or the school board or whomever it was thought we had made a gross error and could not support us. I talked to him in the good times too—when Cody set off for school, and Nevada grew into a young man in high school. I wished for something else—that he could share in what was growing at Community Chest—this abundance of willingness to create programs and services for many in our community and beyond. One time when I was visiting him at his Lake Tahoe house, I handed him my first book. He took it to his chest and held it and said faintly, "There will be more." I did not know this but he did. He knew also that the birth of Community Chest was something neither of us could have planned or foreseen. It was something Debby and I had to do. Out of that necessity we would build the architecture for many people who joined us like he and his colleagues did in Redding. It was faith he conferred, faith from the man who did not have a Western faith, but who had belief, savvy, and desire. Without understanding it at the time, this faith in what we tried to do was sustaining. It was unequivocal, the faith you need to walk alone. I have tried to thank him, to say in poems and stories what this gift of urgent commitment meant but they never quite fulfill the space of his belief in us.

Doubtless this was also true of Lisa. She lived longer than Jess and was able to watch the tiny seed of desire unfold. We were just starting to pay off our building on C Street when Lisa got sick. But it was her mule-headed belief in us, and especially in Debby's uncanny ability to thrive across so many thresholds of people and organizations that sustained us. Sustained us through the long silence of her loss. Like me with Jess, Debby woke endless nights to reach out to her only to find the waiting emptiness. In the way of a healer, her presence, albeit remembered, gave Debby comfort as she was repeatedly tested for trying to lead in our community.

Jess and Lisa had their faults. I will not hide that. But they gave us permission to try something we could only imagine—to build an organization from the ground up. As I said, Debby was not alone but there were many lonely times. Lisa reached into this void without condemnation or judgment. Her resolve gave Debby the strength to go forward when it was most difficult, when she was challenged for doing the smallest thing—and in many cases, the most difficult: advocating for kids in schools and communities. Lisa knew young people better than most. This is what drew them to her and similarly, what drew Debby to her. Lisa expected Debby to go on to make young people the focus of her life. The sorrow of Lisa's move to Hawaii was subsumed by her belief in what Debby could do. She was a shadow presence in her life. Lisa had belief in many things; one of them was Debby.

At night when Debby and I were alone, when the boys were asleep and Shiloh was at our feet, we looked into the darkness of those seven ranges to the east. We wondered who was watching, who was caretaking this dream of ours? Our labor was not enough. We foolishly believed that work alone could sustain us and through effort we could build what until then had only been imagined. Whether the community center or youth programs abroad, they were dreams and only that. We still had no money, no real course forward save the incredible team of board and staff that joined us. But as any non-profit director will tell you, that is not enough. You need something else. You need to know you will persevere. In the darkness of those ridges, they came alive, Lisa and Jess. They lightened this effort with their presence, however small or faint. They listened to our questions, the ones with no answers, the ones that we held out as if to question our very beliefs. This and a thousand other questions they received. In the morning when the boys were up and the dog had been fed, the ridges were closer, almost tangible, and their outlines were clearer, something we could almost touch. This was the way we lived: in the quiet of discussions that never took place save after dark, after peace came to the house.

CHAPTER TWENTY

Forty Words for Brown

Like the Inuit's many variations of the word *snow*, there should be forty words for *brown* to describe every shade from Tonopah to Deeth, every trunk of sage, creosote bush, and bitterbrush blown to dust. There is no language for the brown that seeps in my window. It permeates the eyes and dries the throat. It is on the horizon when I awake and it follows me to the harbor of moonlight when I sleep.

Because there is so little water in this brown land, I must imagine it. Sometimes I mistake the blue light of sky for water. I see trees surrounding the Great Basin, I hear the trickle of creeks, and occasionally pick columbine from the moist earth.

When I am away I wonder what it is like to live with the color green.

Whether it is humid, florid, or alpine, I want to stuff it in my bag and release it when I get off the plane. Even now, writing in this small studio in northern Vermont, I imagine home: the brown beneath our scant snow this winter. It is only when I share pictures that others from far away can see Nevada. They tell me I drove through it once, I went there but it was in search of something else, something like California. We have lived in the shadow of the mother state for a long while and it is all right. I was born there, my parents were also born there and most of my relatives live in the beautiful state. But the beautiful state has irrigation and while much of it is also a desert, it is a desert that is freely chosen.

After years of living here I have learned to choose our desert. When I drive south and east to the bone-scraping town of Mina, the Wild Kat cathouse on its outskirts, four or five marooned Caterpillar tractors, a Studebaker for sale, a bar with two inhabitants, and gas that was once a dollar and sixty-three cents, I began to understand the color brown. It has shaved everything from this community, even the dust has worn its way into the wood. The buildings that still stand are migratory. Soon they will be living beneath the earth. The school, now closed, has an echo of children, and the mine above town has three or four claims on it: something might come from the last exploratory sample. This is the evolution of brown. Dust will take us, dust will return to its rightful place. I keep driving, looking at the sky: is that water overhead, is that the place where moisture meets the sand? The irony, of course, is that the trapped bodies of water, Walker Lake and Pyramid Lake are stunningly beautiful. They are lakes most states would trade mountains for, would empty reservoirs for, and would happily live through drought for. They are beautiful because it is so arid. I have fished in Pyramid when nothing, not even a gull one hundred yards away, could be heard. All that sky was reflected before me, the serrated mountains beyond Anaho Island calling to no one. I imagine what it must have been like at the turn of the century when the fish were so plentiful they were dried for winter food. I imagine hunting rabbits, killing deer, and living in the cold. I imagine trying to outrun the color brown.

Everywhere I turn it finds me: alone in my front yard, rebuilding the fence that blew down again, digging in the rocks and roots of the few pines that understand the driest brown, teasing the grass back to life like it was an altar for our feet, splitting wood that was buried for years in the wood pile, kicking the dirt from the last rounds of oak, wondering if it will burn or if it will simply turn to dust. I lift each piece from the woodpile and load it in the saddle of my weak arm. At the bottom of the rounds, I find some hair and the skeleton of our squirrel, Spike. He lived with us for three years. Every morning he was on top of the wood pile, no matter the weather. Some days he sat on the fence—no more than a half-inch wide. I had not seen Spike for a few months and wondered if he had left in search of food. Before winter, I put seven sunflowers in his den so this made no sense.

Initially I thought he should lie where I found him but then I buried him outside the yard; Sam, our retriever, would dig him up. I buried him in the dirt that was not yet frozen, covered him with rocks so the scavengers would not find him. By then his gray coat had faded, his skeleton was worn, his exact eyes were darkened. I marked the earth with a fence plank that had fallen from the south side of the house. Cedar eaten by wind, dust, and sun. These three were the first settlers of the brown country. They went out in search of a place to hide. They worked slow, swallowed infinite particles of sand. They belonged to a storm of dissatisfaction.

I trace their history across this desert: at the bar in Midas, a frozen dinner comes alive. The gas pump starts, someone has arrived. There is a hitching post outside. Maybe it was a horse that first came here. Paradoxically, there are green trees in the hills above the bar: piñon and juniper. They have adapted to very little water. In the ravine below is the shoe tree, a cottonwood that sprouts tennis shoes from most of its limbs. People throw their discarded Converse and Nikes to die in the wind. The first time I saw them hanging from the tree I thought it was an apparition, a fountain of tennis shoes. Even when you get close it looks like a painting—something from a SoHo loft, not a spectacle of the desert. A spectacle of rubber and cloth decomposing in the sun. If you gas up and head over the pass into the Smith Creek Valley there is a catch-and-release trout pond. It is private, a small dammed body of water. There is a generator that sits back from the house. There is no power in this valley—it is too far from the highway, too far from the lamppost of civilization. If you come here, bring what you need. Bring the staples of survival. Bring water. When you round the next bend three ranches have mailboxes at the highway edge and the dirt roads wind to their doors buckled against the base of the mountain. For the lack of easy electricity, they receive silence in the brown valley. Their alfalfa crop grows in circles because a circular sprinkler irrigates it. After the third cut, it is a field of ochre stems. By winter, it is a solitary brown. If you come back in spring, it is the first sign of contrast—something has prevailed, something has lived to sprout anew. Occasionally, there will be a log cabin falling in on itself, a roof filled with dirt and rock. Coming into Smith Creek Valley a cabin stands by a natural spring, the field is green, the pens set for cattle. Someone ranched here, someone who looked out on thirty miles of cheat grass, sage, and dry land. Someone for whom the color brown was comforting, a guest at the table, in the barn, below the shed. Their tools were wrapped in dust, their fingers cleaned of dirt twice a day before meals. Someone whose spouse had to learn to love this color, had to forget what she left—the weather that drove her away. Drove her to the back of a horse, to a ranch in the middle of the desert. They invented a story to stay here: harvest, heat, fire, dry, brittle, shade, shadow, storm, wind, moon. They did not bring enough blankets. They read the clouds to plant, irrigate, and prepare. They belonged to the weather, conscripted to the ruts that led them to this valley. These are our ancestors, those who met the color brown. They grew up in this valley, but we have inherited their rituals. We have grown used to the hash mark on the horizons—the yellow borderline of Utah, the green fields of Oregon, the alpenglow of the Sierra Nevada, and to the south, the final eclipse of the Mojave Desert. We are defined by what is missing—water, trees, and vegetation—so that by being here we are part of the color itself. Our skin becomes dry, the pigment darkens. We reflect the light outside. We find the precise word to describe the auburn light of a windy day, the olive light of a coming storm, the unyielding light of a dust devil. We answer each day with the whitened hand of a petroglyph. We surrender to the atmosphere.

Occasionally, when a car drives by I am startled: others have come this way, but mostly I drive in silence. In the evenings when I come home from Lovelock, Winnemucca, Tonopah, I recite the preamble of stars. Sometimes there is a moon rising at my back, fed from a spring of orange light. I have pulled over to watch it rise, cast a shadow on the hot springs in the alkali fields. When Debby and I first came to this valley those ponds kept us warm and the moon was something I had never seen: a luminous globe of hot color. Even now, the moonrise is a new chapter in the night, a partial circle poking from the clouds to the east. Although I cannot say why, its beauty is tied to the loss of daylight, the eternal close of day. I'm sure the moisture from other skies has faded into this darkness so that the moon has nothing left to hide. It opens the desert to the feral kingdom of night birds and predators—all those who wait for the hour to hunt. At night the desert is a lunar landscape—the deep beds of sand, of endless space with little contrast, and the sudden outcropping of rocks, also foreign to the eye. Driving Highway 50, I try to read the many epitaphs for love: Danny, I need you. Billy, come home. Darla, where are you? All these epigrammatic lines written with rocks on the desert floor. By the time I reach Fallon the last planes touch down at the Naval Air Station and the night-light is free again. Lake Lahontan ripples in the pooled light. A fisherman waits for the nibble of smallmouth bass. I wonder if it is my old friend Jess in the boat. I wonder if I will see him when I disappear in the moonlight. The cottonwoods struggle along the shore. This has been a dry winter—their roots are normally underwater, but tonight they are exposed. We are all exposed in this light. When I get to Six Mile Canyon the moonlight is at my back, a follower, dodging in and out of the trees. The trickle at the road edge is from the treatment pond, and the owl that I hear from my porch readies for the hunting hour. If there is any comfort in this light, it is the *whooo, whooo, whooo,* of his breath, a great horned owl no doubt. He has lived below me for years and even though I can't see him, he sings the note of captivity: I must eat, I must eat. Once, at the petroglyphs, we came upon two baby great horned owls in a knot in a cottonwood tree. I almost missed them but Debby whispered, "Come here—look!" They were so small in the darkness. All I could see was their eyes in the pointy hair. Then I saw their mother, thirty feet away, as big an owl as I have seen. Haunting and skillful, I thought she would come at us, chase us from the nest. We walked away slowly, having been given the gift of their presence: two five-inch Kachina dolls, just awakened to the specter of people larger than tree limbs. When I hear that great horned owl moan at the top of Six Mile Canyon I remember riding my bike on a winter day and coming upon the wings of a bird frozen in a puddle at the road's edge. I chipped at the ice—a great horned owl that must have been blinded by an oncoming car. I rode home with it and called the wildlife authorities. No one would take it; it was endangered. But it was already dead, surely someone could use it—a museum, a school, an ornithologist? My bird would not leave the garage. I spread its wings on a piece of plywood and let the mites do their work. In the summer the feathers were a full bloom of brown and gray and auburn hues. The eyes had hollowed to witness the heat of summer. The garage was always too hot because I did not ventilate it properly. But the bird stayed on the bench for three summers and winters until I let it go, let it persist in the moonlight. This is what I hear driving home. This is who accompanies me. This is what I have come to rely on: the sound of an owl. This is what I say to the light at my back: follow me, follow me home. Let me rest in the bed of our room with no curtains. Let me find sleep when the light is brightest at 3 A.M. Let me wake in the wild canopy of light over and over so that I can remember its passage into morning, into my hands when the red sun becomes a blister and I relinquish my fear of living with the color brown.

On train to Gold Hill, L-R Nevada, Lisa Griffin
(Shaun's sister), Cody, and Debby, 1990
by Shaun Griffin

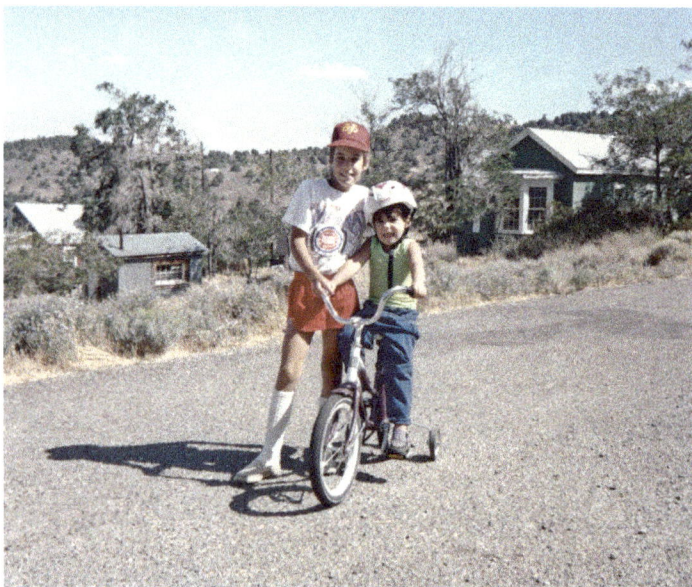

Cody on bicycle with Nevada standing, K Street house, Virginia City, 1992
by Debby Loesch-Griffin

K Street Griffin house, Virginia City, 1992
by Shaun Griffin

Sugar Loaf, Virginia City, 1992
by Shaun Griffin

Second Community Chest office, C Street, Virginia City, 1995
by Shaun Griffin

Fire just east of Virginia City, 1998
by Shaun Griffin

Community Center, Virginia City, 2011
by Shaun Griffin

Community Center, Virginia City, 2011
by Shaun Griffin

III

CHAPTER TWENTY-ONE

Passing Through Nevada

I have tracked this light through two decades of weather and now the sun is low in the southern sky. The rabbit brush burns to seed and the first wood fires fill the air. Snow came last week and Debby brought the green tomatoes inside to ripen in the window. To the east, the sky is auburn to the Stillwater Range.

Days ago, Debby and I drove the width of the state to a poetry reading at the Border Inn. The clouds followed us coming and going, spotted the desert floor with patches of light, then dark. There is little to define such expanse—the eyes have a separate kingdom in which to declare beauty: each valley receded deeper and deeper into the horizon. The flanks of mountains were like caves. And always, two crows were at the roadside.

In Austin, we had a blackberry shake at the Toiyabe Café and climbing out of the small town, the aspens were like leaf-fire on the ridges. But it was as if no one had driven this road, as if it was empty of human footprints. There was only light and distance to mark our passage through the Great Basin.

I came to western edge of the Great Basin in 1978, ignorant of light and shadow, of the wind that hails in all seasons. But standing at the base of Wheeler Peak, eight hours from my home, elevation 10,000, I was also home. At that elevation, the aspens and the soft woods were candles in the evergreens. Wheeler had a dusting of snow and the ice below had not melted over the summer. There were ferns, wildflowers, does, and streambeds. It was idyllic in every sense and the bristlecones, icons of survival in this land, stood gnarled and bent, the last word in a geography of silence.

I wished to take it with me—this peace of the high altitude. I wished to take my boys up the trailhead again and find the note we stuffed in a crack of granite at the summit. No doubt the wind had eaten it and the paper was blown to the valley below.

That night I read with musicians and poets from the Snake Valley, fifteen performers from Baker and beyond. A miracle of art is that it needs no home. It can appear in any landscape, at any moment. Days later, my friend the writer and jazz musician Bob Reid would perform the debut of his "Bristlecone Mass" in Carson City—inspired by words from Black Elk: a tree would shelter us, provide for us, bring our story to its most elemental—concern for one another. We would find rest beneath its cover. His choral performance was a prayer, an offering for us to unite beneath a symbol, a bristlecone. Whether tree or station, Baker or Carson, there was a reason for doing more than passing through this land.

I have passed through many borders, real and imagined, broken time from its consequence of days and known throughout it all the record of subtle survival: this basin and range has held us. My archeologist neighbor tells me the Clovis Culture was here at least 14,000 years ago. I cannot begin to understand what they saw or heard in the vast boundary of burnt mountains or what hunger measured their daily routine.

Today, for some, it is not much different. This highway that bisects the state is a path through many communities, but the resources are scarce and the distance to commerce is daunting. We are in a modern time, but the chaste requirements of living here have not changed, nor I imagine, has the light. It is said that the clearest sky in North America is in Tonopah, in the center of the state, because there is little light pollution. I was in Tonopah this week, a town made from mining, but now solar power fuels the jobs, a resource they can use without worry of reclamation. The consequent excitement was palpable: the Mizpah Hotel reopened. The community had reason to hope that this place would become a possible future for its children. Driving the last hour from Mina, the rain poured down, nearly blinding my vision. Rain—in this dry place—an episodic reversal of fortune. There were puddles at the road edge and sage that had been dry for seven months was in pools of brown runoff. The persons I met with said they couldn't recall such a storm. It, too, altered the light to a parallel horizon: the crack in the clouds above the valley floor gave two views. A panorama of seeing, of color with fresh definition. The desert remains unfinished, a place of perpetual motion, but it is in the light that I first notice this change.

In this autumn of burnished lines, the roads east and south converge on a limitless sky out my door. When you live in a place for a long time, first impressions fade to memory as if they were stored under glass. But the light has grown more distinct, taught me to pay attention to its abundant presence. The poet Joanne de Longchamps wrote of the similarity of light in Greece and Nevada. Greece is a country of supreme cultural history whose light is breathtaking. In Nevada we have no Parthenon, no obvious source of cultural definition, but it is not a made culture that sustains many who live here. It is something subtler, more difficult to articulate and why, I imagine, it is often passed through. The feral sounds, the isolated ridge top beauty are easily missed which further exacerbates the perception that nothing is here.

I did not know the depth of this place when I came to Virginia City. I learned it, especially now, in the time of cutting wood, of leaf fall. I learned it because I had to know where I lived, to understand the darkest light of an imminent storm and the perfect dawn of a storm passed. In other words, to stay here I had to learn what was made without me, without any of us, a practice of mind the Buddhists undertake. I was raised a noisy Presbyterian. Thought of this order required silence. Even now, decades into its ordination, I am a student, a novice who can begin to appreciate the three antelope who stood in our path to Baker, the bighorn sheep on the cliffs above Walker Lake, or the bobcat kit who crossed before me on Geiger Summit.

If this was my first day I would stand where I am now, at the rock wall on the southern side of our house, and listen: starlings, quail, piñon jay—the noisemakers—and then return to the other senses that define a place. It is still warm in the October sun but the nights are near freezing. The spruce buds and cornflowers are dying. Soon the light will be whitened and the night, a story of stars. I might say on this first day what brown fields lie to the east, might invoke a separate knowledge to understand who was left in this place, and who, without knowledge, kept on. I might draw a picture to represent the climb up Mt. Davidson out my back door, the pole raised on its peak to signify a century of living below, the USGS stamp marking its coordinates on the map. I might raise my head to find a universe of light and shadow and pretend I was the first to see it. And yet, I would not know its sour dust on my tongue. I would not know its harsh wind at my ears, its breath of thousands of miles pulsing at my skin. I would, however, know I was alone on my first day in this place and it would be an intimate knowledge, shared with the person I would meet out of necessity. Of course, I am only guessing. I lived for years without the rudiments of what was required. I make no promise they are understood now. Still, on this first day, I would thank what careful and constant forces led to this geographic upheaval, this mutiny of mountains and bare land, almost opaque in the distance. I would bend to the ground and release my fingers in the leaves, raise my head as if I had come to harvest its light.

CHAPTER TWENTY-TWO

Pushing to Meet the Need

Like most people who work, I bring many selves to this labor of building a community: the poet, the father, the teacher and yet they are never enough. The task is always greater than my cumulative strength. I depend on many people. They are the threshold for my understanding: together we move in consort. It is far more difficult to include than isolate, but it is necessary. Until I had to rely on others to finish the center I made very little progress. When I was pushed to extremes by circumstance or politics, there was nothing to thwart the fear of endeavor. I needed help, and mostly in the form of belief—now more than ever: the board had asked me to proceed on a dream. Build it. It was coming on sixteen years since we sat down with Art and the five young people. *Build it*—in 2009 those words were like clouds of threat and promise.

More urgent than the revenue was the omnipresent need: our two high school programs for at-risk youth had outgrown the confines of the four computer stations in the office. The kids were literally using all of the main floor space for their school work—the kitchen, the Classroom on Wheels and counseling offices, and waiting room. This made for tight quarters and lots of noise. Similarly, the before- and after-school program had grown to thirty students in a cramped cafeteria. There was no time for the janitorial staff to strip the floors and wax them for the coming year because it was used for the entire summer. The staff had to be extra creative to devise programs that would challenge multi-grade youth in an echo chamber. When they walked to the pool, it was a train of lunch pails and towels. Safety became more and more of an issue—if something were to happen while the kids walked the three hundred yards to the pool it would have severe repercussions.

I added and re-added the numbers—Senator Reid obtained a final $194,000 and the new health center promised $150,000. If we cut back on the building, trimmed wherever possible, and started with what we had—$680,000, we might be able to complete the shell and one-half of the downstairs. I had little choice but to present this option to the board, the commissioners, and the community: if I did not act soon, the terms of the lease would be unmet and the first federal appropriation from Reid would have to be returned. This took another year of presentations, discussion, and planning. During this time the architect and his partner drafted a call for proposals and they, my wife, and I interviewed several qualified applicants. This was all done predicated on the belief that we would get approval. We made a decision and went with a local construction company—they understood what was at stake.

Of course I could not sign any contract until the commissioners and my board gave approval. This process took most of the summer and by September, I signed my name on a contract that was two inches thick and obligated me to more money than I had seen.

Two months later one of the funders pulled out—their deputy director lied about their contribution to the project. I had less than six months to replace the revenue—all the while watching the building take form. At the same time, the state's budget went into an ever deeper spiral, and again I was torn between choosing one source of revenue for the office and one for the center. We lost more than $100,000 in that budget year—a tenth of our revenue (excluding the center). I did not know where to turn: I had repeatedly asked the foundation and public sources for contributions. At last, I returned to the two foundations that believed in us from the beginning—again, they offered matching grants of $50,000 and $25,000 to finish the building. In the interim, a close friend and novelist told me of his friend who had worked on several foundation requests. We met and mapped out a strategy to raise the remaining $250,000. We sent three proposals off— nothing happened to the first one, the second responded with a partial contribution, and the third was almost surreal. In less than a week after sending the request, the director met with me on site for one-half hour. Five days later we received word: they would contribute $75,000. This happened because many well-known individuals and personal friends joined hands to make this *their* project. By then other foundations wanted to participate: one asked me to resubmit an application to join this effort. They contributed $25,000 and another did the same thing. It became an honor to be involved with the evolution of this building. It stood for more than a place for youth and families—meaning, it was a shared ideal. One donor said, "We've almost finished building *our* center."

* * *

I drove back from Winnemucca yesterday in harsh wind. The sky was a cloud of brown and gray. A storm threatened but this dust, alkali and sand, was an inglorious mixture of particles so thick I could not see more than a half-mile ahead. In the morning I had driven by a serious accident and the image of the twisted cars stayed with me. There was a black sheet on the highway where the body would lie. All of us slowed but it did no good: the wind had its say. As I drove past the trucks, we struggled to keep our lane. More than one of us wondered if the sirens would follow.

Outside of Silver Springs the snow started. By then the cloud was black—it hid the late afternoon sun and began to stick. The desert valley rarely has snow and when it comes it is gone in a day. I still had to climb up Six Mile Canyon, the twisting two-lane to home. I wondered if the accident had cleared. When I arrived at the ridge there were skid marks. A man walked on the bluff of the road. A car followed above him. He held his face. It must have been a family member trying to grieve in this most unforgiving cold. The wind was no healer, no arbiter of peace on the highway. In the morning I would read why: a young person with alcohol. The twin coils of demise. All I could think of was the wind and that man staggering in the sage, trying to say goodbye to his loved one.

At dinner I remembered Sarah Winnemucca, daughter of the Paiute chief for whom the town was named. Maybe it was the snow or the young woman lost in the wreckage but I couldn't shake the image of Sarah, buried to her neck in that same cold desert, a fourteen year-old girl hidden beneath a piece of sage, waiting for the return of her tribe. This was during the mid-1800s when the West was scavenged. Her family buried her to keep her from being killed—which is why we know her story today. Ancestor of the highway, of blowing dust and light, I wished she were here to comfort that man, to help him find his way back.

This morning I returned to Jeff Nicholson's gallery. He has taken the painting *Evening Shadows Across Nevada* home. "I have to finish the air. It is very hard to paint air—." The air I saw yesterday threatens and chafes. It is like a blister welling up beneath the skin. This is air that wants to be outside of art, air that lies alongside the road, near the feet of those it has abandoned. He will bring something into the gallery I have not seen: a worry of air and light at the bend in the land. The air on which we tread.

*   *   *

Four months into construction of the center my colleague calls to say Congress has stripped his project from the federal budget for the coming year. The center was designed around its health services. All of the necessary infrastructure was in the building—plumbing, electrical, office design—and now, poof, it may not be realized if the Senate approves the cut. Many people are concerned. They want to know what will replace it. They want to know if it will be replaced. They want to know how we will proceed. I do not have answers, any more than I have the crystal ball to finish the center. Yesterday, in Winnemucca, I asked another donor for the funds to finish this phase—$75,000. That is all I can understand at this point. The tomorrow of other plans has been scuttled. The land beneath shifted. I must adapt and do what I can to finish this building—finish the air, as Jeff Nicholson said. The air that is incomplete. It is the only concrete knowledge I have: finish the structure. Once we do, we will take stock. Living without certainty has given me permission to act: this is what we must do. Finish. The result of the mantra the board gave me eighteen months ago: build it.

*   *   *

In one week, we will hold the grand opening. Half of the lower floor will be finished. Many people are ecstatic we have reached this milestone. A beautiful article came out in the local paper—a picture of the center was on the front page. Today, Debby and I went to the copy store to record a glimpse of this history for Art, the architect. A headline from the same paper seventeen years ago: "Community Center Inches Forward." Below that, the first plans he drew eighteen years ago. We will give this framed record of his journey with pictures of the five young people—all grown now— to him at the event. When it is over, Debby and I will walk out into the night and imagine a new future, something not yet done. Something with which to remember the next twenty years.

*   *   *

At the snowy grand opening four of the five original students returned (one could not make it because the Sierra pass had closed). When they spoke Art could not hide his gratitude. He and his architectural partner, Darrin, wept openly. All of them went over to Art and spoke to him sitting by the podium. He was unsteady on his feet but determined to be there, to witness this moment. Each of the young people told of their dream for such a place, and now, with most of them out of college, it would be the place where the next generation would gather. Even though they hinted at the gift Art had given them, he would defer: it was they who had given him their friendship. This was a man whose architecture wove people together.

Debby and I never imagined Art would coach us through the building of the center. For most of the time, the path to its creation was not in view. All that we could see was born in a classroom with five young people. It was nothing more than a drawing on paper, nothing more than an idea in the long succession of ideas that define adolescence. Yet, this one took hold of us, of them, and Art began, slow at first, in his indubitable manner, to prepare. When Debby and I most needed reassurance that this was not a wholly unthinkable proposition, he listened and offered specific suggestions. Although there was nothing concrete to show for our progress, he designed a building that *was* beautiful and functional—an anathema to skeptics and a way forward to its supporters.

Art still defers when asked how the center got built. He walks three miles most mornings with his dog. We see each other in a restaurant or at a jazz club and acknowledge what has been done with a handshake. What we want is more time together. What we inevitably find is this day and tomorrow if we are lucky. He might stare at me from the reception at a funeral of a mutual friend. He might ask for a hand with his notebook on the way out the door. He might signal that he cannot speak and swallow at the same time. He has a tremor. Always frugal with time, he motions to return to the desk and I oblige. There is work to be done.

CHAPTER TWENTY-THREE

Stepping Outside the Prison

Virginia City, 1999: Nevada answered the door to Stan, one of the men who had been in the poetry workshop with me since its inception. This experience repeated itself in the coming years. Never certain of anything, the men walked from the yard.

Stan and Ella stood on the porch. We walked outside—it was June, the lilacs were in bloom. Stan stood at the picket fence: "This is the first time I have looked at a sky without razor wire in eleven-and-a-half years." He touched everything—pine needles, grass, irises, and especially our dog, Shiloh, a golden lab. We walked in the house and I made eggs benedict. The plates were colorful, remnants from our days in graduate school when Carolyn Kizer, a poet who helped edit my first book, picked them out for Debby. Now they circled the table. There were knives and forks, not just spoons. Stan ate in silence. He was overwhelmed with emotion. He had not walked up stairs, opened a door, chosen what to eat, or sat on a wooden chair in over a decade.

When he was still inside I visited his room that had four other men in it. It had so little light I could barely see the walls of the building. But this was a privilege—he was not sleeping in a cell.

He had done enough time that he could live with extra books, soft music, and a handful of mementos above his bed. His girlfriend, Ella, visited him for more than five years. Occasionally, she brought her son who was fourteen at the time. Stan wanted to be a surrogate father. Stan wanted to try everything on that day he walked out of prison. It was a short drive to our house: his first ride in a car, his first ride next to a woman, his first sensation of speed and flesh. In the backyard, I made some offhand remark about picking up dog poop. Stan said, "I'd pick up dog poop all day."

He kept looking at the color in our living room, the paintings of the wide-open expanse we live in. I am sure his retina was trying to process some color other than denim, steel, or the color men live in to survive. Cody kept asking Stan, "This is the first time you have held a glass in ten years? The first time you have hugged a dog? That's as long as I've been alive." Stan just nodded and smiled. Ella said very little. I think both of them thought the entire morning was surreal, something you dream about for years and then one day, it happens. There was no key, no dress code, and no surveillance. Cody was his happy self: "When can I go outside? Do you want to ride my bike? I can show you how—," and he was gone before Stan could answer.

The slow-motion morning of awakening was spinning into midday. They had a long drive ahead to another state, the first of many before they would reach the other coast. I knew they were anxious to leave and yet they could have stayed for hours. It was like stopping time—seeing these memories return to their faces. The future had many things waiting but it also had worry: they could get pulled over, something could go wrong, and something could be said. I tried to assure him that today was a beginning. All he wanted was more of the senses, the intoxicating return of everything that had been missing. We strung balloons on the fence and they were floating in the wind. Stan held one of them at the gate, pressed it to his face: "I'm going home now," he said and pulled it from the string and handed it to Nevada. I hugged Stan and Ella, closed her car door and watched them drive out of view. I knew the highway would be long, but I knew also they would not care if it took weeks to arrive.

On my trips to the East for work, Stan would drive to see me. He slept on the hotel floor, told me about his job, his family, and I listened. He had fallen off the wagon a few times but was back in AA. Ella was the first casualty of the tension in the family business, but they are friends. He still tries to be a father to her son. He remembers something of the day he walked into our yard and my son answered the door. He is off parole now and another decade has passed. Even though there is much that is imperfect about his situation, he is free. He lives with the repercussions of his past each day and they remind him over and over: this is not who you are.

*　　　　　*　　　　　*

Johnny was released in 2013 when I was out of state. Of all the places, we met at a Starbucks three days later. It was January and the interior was lit up with music and busy people. When Johnny was sentenced, cell phones, computers, and fancy coffee houses were not the norm. Johnny was inside for twenty-nine years, long enough to Braille the contents of the most recent *Razor Wire,* the journal from the workshop. I couldn't hold the camera still to record this moment for him, for us. I knew it would slip away to the coming weeks of searching for work. He was as ebullient as I have seen him, and in the twenty-four years he was in the workshop, we saw each other through many highs and lows. He could not account for the present that he found himself in and certainly not the nearly three decades spent inside, but he was relatively young at fifty-two and had every hope of making poetry and art on the outside. He had so many dreams: finish college, find a meaningful job, reconnect with his family, and when he finally had an apartment, start painting and writing again.

His sister came up from Southern California to meet him when he got out. She spent the day getting the essentials—clothes, phone, and DMV paperwork to apply for an ID card. After she left I called him for a week before he found out—he had no idea how to program voice mail. Without a car, he spent 3-4 hours a day on the bus looking for work. He made numerous phone calls to the VA, the community college, and the bank only to discover the new world lived on-line. At night he returned to the halfway house and attended twice-weekly AA groups.

He took a ceramics class at the community college from my good friend and sculptor Tom Turman. He had never touched clay but the human body became one of many perspectives: light, form, and consequence. Johnny was lucky: he had many artists pulling for him and Tom was one of them. By the end of the semester Tom told me Johnny was the most talented student he had taught. Strong words but they were not unexpected.

I watched Johnny create the cover art for fourteen issues of *Razor Wire,* watched him use pastel, watercolor, and pen and ink for his signature "scribbles." His acrylic painting had an almost photographic quality to it—he could recreate the emotion in a face from a photograph in a magazine or newspaper with an eerie accuracy.

Within a month of his release, Johnny and I went to visit two other artists—Nolan Preece and Tom Gilbertson, both of whom had shown his artwork in Sun Mountain Artworks. Tom owned the gallery first and later sold it to Nolan. It was a fixture of Virginia City art and artists for almost a decade. It was also the home of the Comstock Arts Council in the late '90s. Both men held openings for each new issue of *Razor Wire* and helped me organize the shows. I called all of my friends to read from the journal—Gailmarie Pahmeier, Gary Short, the late Bill Cowee, Tom Meschery, Emma Sepúlveda and other poets. In time, they began to know the work of the men in the workshop. All of them except Bill came into the workshop to teach class and they hoped that reading the work of the poets brought them life outside of prison.

I met Johnny's sister at one of the readings. She was with another sister and her husband. At that time the prospect of his release seemed ephemeral. As the years clicked by, she would call to prepare for the day he would step from prison. I cautioned her against getting her hopes up and said I would do the same with him because stepping out of prison is little more than an idea when time becomes the bargaining chip in one's life.

Johnny is a deeply talented artist, but like Stan, he was not prepared for the repeated frustration at the temp agencies, the burger joints, and the delivery jobs. When his sister found him a car, he finally got a graveyard job at a warehouse. It was punishing physical labor and within weeks he was pounding 8-10 Advil a shift. He asked for three days off to take a photography workshop from Nolan Preece. They said you can go and keep on going.

Nolan spent years mastering Chemigrams, a technique using common photo chemistry to form an image on photographic paper or other silver-based photographic material without a camera and under room light. Johnny made an image of himself stepping out of a weathered picture frame with the contents of one his poems in the background. Nolan asked him how he tipped the image of his self-portrait into the Chemigram to give it a collage effect. It wasn't that it hadn't been done; rather, Johnny imagined it as something that *could* be done with Chemigrams.

It was clear to me and the other artists that what he needed most was art. He did have one thing that could not be taken away from the relentless job search—his manuscript. I watched those poems be born thorn by thorn, over more than two decades. The poems haunted me when I read them for the first time and they do so now. The book is divided into three sections: his youth, family, and prison. There is no distraction from the consequence of his life inside, and that is what led another dear friend, Robert Blesse, the former director of Black Rock Press, to publish them.

To my dismay, he left this area to live with his sister. It was the only way he could stay alive—taking care of two adult family members with disabilities for a meager sum. He wants to return to college and now has a fine Chicano poet rooting for him, with whom he may study. When his book was published he had to get special permission from his parole officer to return to Nevada to read from it. Even though the evening went long and he read last, people were sobbing, awestruck by the authenticity of his poems. Whatever poetry you believe in, his is irrefutable. Like Stan, I hope to hear from him until I can no longer hear, but if I do not, I hope his art has allowed him to live without looking over his shoulder.

CHAPTER TWENTY-FOUR

The Echo Skittering Through Town

Mid-May and there is no reprieve from the snow. It's almost spring of 2012. Yesterday we gardened in the brief window of sun, afraid the cold would return, and then white flakes came this morning. Later we were in the Silver City studio of the painter Karen Kreyeski to see her new series of oils on Death Valley. They were on fiberboard so the contours of color and landscape were particularly lush. She titled one of the paintings *Licorice Canyons*. One of the paintings was of my neighbor and teacher, Ric Schrank, cycling the dry ridges of the desert highway. Like Death Valley, the Comstock is a place where artists sculpt the ancient boundaries of wind and water. Her studio is light and the windows face south but today the wind drove us inside. How did we come to live by the weathervane? The few green flowers that poke from her rock bed are shrines to what might be a warm day. Although a longtime resident, she paints as if she needs this hardened land.

She lives near the painters Jeff Nicholson and his wife, Jean LeGassick. When I last left his gallery he wondered if he could leave this place—not because he loved it any less but rather, the talk skittering through town: a mine was coming. An open sore where we live. What did we have to stop it? Not much, not even the relic of our history. He and Jean wanted to retire and move to Surprise Valley but their house had dropped in value—a consequence of things to come.

Now friends call: will I join the fight? Which one, I want to ask? The one for the greater good, the one to stop the next speculator from digging, or the one to feed or clothe the lone homeless woman who walks our clapboard town night and day in any weather?

Many years ago, a D-8 Caterpillar stunned our close friends the Wesners when they lived in Gold Hill, just above the Houston Minerals Pit. It was going to bulldoze their access road to begin excavation in the cavernous hole behind their house. Had Ben not confronted the driver, the yellow earthmover would have gone right down their road and left them in a pool of dust. The driver seemed completely at ease with his work—moving what he was told—earth from one place to another. His face was impenetrable: shades, hat, and whiskers. There was little to feign interest. He left the diesel idling for hours, certain he was on the right path. An injunction followed and soon the Cat was stalled. This is the echo skittering through town. This has happened at least five times in my three decades on the Comstock. The companies promise more than they deliver and when the speculation dries up, they disappear, only to leave yet another pockmark on the land.

Now they want to dig between Devil's Gate and the southern boundary of Virginia City—maybe a half-mile in circumference and 800 feet deep. Gold is at an all-time high, who can blame them? Who except painters like Jeff and Jean whose house has lost its value? Who except those of us who live here, the hundreds of citizens of Silver City, Gold Hill, and southern Virginia City? Debby was a counselor for some of their children after she left the alternative high school. Most mornings she picked up the young girls en route to Dayton High School. One went on to become a filmmaker, another a chef, still another a non-profit director. Their parents are actors, house painters, archeologists, photographers, contractors and writers. People we have known for thirty years.

These are not imagined people. These are people with whom we have tilled this landscape, cherished one another's children, and charted our own small existences in this place—through planning committees, school boards, commissioners, volunteer fire departments, and a hundred other nameless activities that put faces on our P.O. boxes. Somehow, because the shovels that repeatedly come for the gold are itinerant, the presumption is made that we must also be without roots on this already honeycombed mountain.

Then their marketing team calls me: "Well, Shaun, it's for the benefit of the community—jobs, taxes, charity—this will be a game changer." Two days ago a market researcher phoned to determine how I felt about the mine. I couldn't tell who employed them; the questions were quaintly neutral.

When I read *Roughing It* to Cody he was about ten and the book seemed comical, farcical, a wild ride through the West of what it was purported to be in most points east of here. Penny stocks grew overnight to unheard-of value, and a new hole became a strike almost daily. The news spread to San Francisco. Everyone took the spoils, and then it went away, as fast as it arrived. From 15,000 people to 10,000 to less than 1,000 today. Twain was right about the humor: the joke was on us. But back then, there was not a community here, save the Washoe and the Paiute who were chased from these ridges. It was a place that could be exploited; there was nothing to worry over, no debt to repay. That is why the book is such a harbinger: no doubt the gold diggers will return. Remember them for their earnest desire to improve the quality of life in your small town.

A mining executive from one of the largest commercial gold companies in the world told me the geography doesn't support this speculation. The major gold veins are in northeastern Nevada— where the largest companies have multiple mines and employ many thousands to extract its gold. That is quite unlike building a new pit in the middle of the largest historic district in the country. There is a community here. We have worked decades to build one, to put in place the kinds of structures that support healthy children and families: schools, ballparks, youth programs and the promise of a future. What is it about the future these youth look forward to? Home, family, and land that will support them in their adult years. The irony is that this speculation will never touch the futures of those who come with shovels. They recently had a stockholders' meeting in Gold Hill. The residents picketed their meeting and they were predictably shunned. Not because they were "flies" on the wall but, rather, the investors might be led to believe that this was "unwise" for their portfolios. There is a further irony: the two counties that abut this mine, Storey and Lyon, need the revenue and speculation is strong temptation. If this sounds like *Roughing It*, it is, of course, because even Twain would be laughing to learn it is happening all over again in the same place, to the same people's descendants, with the same small consequence of greed. When gold drops to $1,000 or $250 an ounce like it was in the last decade, this will become a curious bi-product of living in the West: what one must do for a living when the land is left alone.

Mining is not what's wrong; it is a part of our cultural history, but there is a middle ground. Before a decision to go forward is made the people who will be most affected by digging an open pit should be the mine's first consideration.

Next week there will be a vote on a special use permit for the proposed exploratory drilling, and later the same process will take place in Lyon County. People will be affected by their decision—their livelihoods and neighborhoods will depend on it. If this were only fiction, even the hyperbolic journalism of Twain's time, it might seem palatable, but it is nothing short of real. Somewhere I have read that there is no place left to run. This is *The Last Best Place* as William Kittredge and Annick Smith have written of their beloved Montana, and we must abide its formidable requirements for survival: what comes in the name of money demands scrutiny. We have ample examples of what has left in the name of its loss. Nothing is clean or clear in the boardrooms of American business. Neither is it here where we live and work and play, but the two may co-exist without the threat of excess to guide our decisions. We can find a middle ground that allows this community to thrive and retains some underground mining.

*   *   *

What remains unsaid troubles most: those who get caught in this web. The hustlers, the down-and-outers for whom personal responsibility is living on the sidelines. When they call me to ask what I want for the non-profit, I am chagrined. How much money will it take to sway my decision? The implicit understanding is this will further our work. Perhaps an anonymous donation might assuage my conscience but I doubt it will do much for the residents nearest the digging. The sad truth is this is an allegory for so many communities—when dollars take precedence over people the community spirals downward. Nevada is threaded with boom and bust communities. Today they look quaint—curious byproducts of times past. The clapboard buildings falling down, the tailings, and the pits circled in barbed wire. This is our history but it is a history of plunder. Yes jobs were created and they will be created again, but the resource is finite and when it is gone the people will leave.

This is where we started to build a community that is not dependent on the ebb and flow of precious metal prices. The West is a checkerboard of balance and discovery, trust and deceit, water and aridity. Fueled by its scarce resources, we continue to believe the improbable can happen again: there is just enough to get rich and leave. This speculation could never happen in a densely populated area but here, where it is endlessly open, there is a perception that the land is forgiving and will replenish itself. Perhaps, and perhaps we will be here when it does, but in the interim, what balance remains will take all of us—left, right and center—to protect it.

*　　　　　*　　　　　*

There were over 300 people at the hearing for the special use permit. Friends on both sides testified, and people who will surely profit had charts and diagrams. The hunt was on, they told us. More than five hours later the issue was tabled. More research was needed. It is not the research I am worried about; it is the sphere of influence, the permission to discuss what cannot be seen: how this community will change. When they leave, and they surely will, the dust will again subside and the residents will move on to the task at hand: rebuilding the land that was left behind. This should come as no surprise—the angel of remorse is the last to sign off on such things. Still, I want us to do better. I want our children to return and discover what was right about this place. The past is an imperfect teacher; we shepherd its commentary like it was put up in canning jars for long days of winter reflection. But when the sun returns as it finally has now, it is hard to run from the consequence of our decisions.

We had a late summer this year—rain and snow for much of June, but that gave us the rare and unmatched beauty of July with cornflowers, Chinese poppies, hollyhocks and wild roses, all imported from those who came to the Comstock. It is quiet and deeply blue on the horizon. The seven ridges out my window remind me of eternal time, a landscape unknown, undiscovered and unbelievably green before the Sierra Nevada rose up to stop the moisture from the west. This is a constant reminder of our place in this vast and burnished land. To some eyes, it has no utility and therefore is empty, but like Mark Strand said of poetry, you must slow down for it. So, too, must the high desert be seen on its own terms. The slow reach of time requires us to pay attention: the land will change without notice, but if we are careful in our living, it may yet prosper, may yet cultivate new civilizations, new eras of timekeeping.

The echo skittering through town will die down, the boardrooms will move on to the next best thing. We will return to the edge of this mountain with some measure of hope for the future. In this, we have little choice: the land was scarred long ago. We have been rebuilding what was left for the past century—even a steam locomotive to bring tourists to this place on the trestles and bridges from Carson. That is how we understand our relationship to this ground: it is not sacred but it is home. We take pride in it and for a few months every year it almost looks like a Victorian town with lawns, flowers and a handful of trees that persist without water—locust, tree of heaven, piñon, and juniper—something like green beyond the patios and porches of the thousand residents of Virginia City. When the snow returns it is hard and harsh, easy to imagine a place of no inhabitants.

But that would be a ruse: no one wants the town to disappear and that may yet keep us from digging for riches.

I have been told many times in many hearings to trust the process. I heard it repeated again in the hearing last week. What I trust is the dignity and good will of my neighbors and friends, people for whom this town is a place of compromise: for the peace of living at 6,200 feet, you belong to its future and heed its boundaries of arid sacrifice. You do what is necessary to husband the miracle of its gift.

CHAPTER TWENTY-FIVE

Looking Through the Tourists

They have been spotted everywhere—parked in the middle of the road, on the hilltop corners coming into town, in restaurants, churches, and private houses—cameras in hand, hoping to find the people who once lived here. When they stop in the middle of C Street at the lone flashing light, our car behind them, we can only hope our brakes work well enough to sustain their gaze. When I'm in the post office, they quietly ask, "Does anybody live here?" as if superstition had spooked all real people from the town. "Surely this is a ghost town," and I smile acknowledging their humble observations. "Do people still carry guns?" they ask as the wanna-be cowboys walk by, six shooters holstered at their side.

They descend on the town once the weather warms and they leave at the first hint of snow. The merchants live and die by them, which makes for interesting times—about six months of little work, followed by a summer of fairly reckless camera hicks, so that when the camels arrive, the motorcycles arrive, or the outhouses arrive, we know it's almost over. In truth, most of the tourists are here to see the place that "grew up on *Bonanza*," but has nothing to do with

Hoss and Little Joe. On a good day I can hear six, seven languages on the wooden boardwalk. I can't think of a smaller town that is more widely visited than Virginia City but the tourists hate the road in any weather. It's not uncommon to see them completely stopped on a blind curve coming up from or back down to Reno. They must be the only person driving this treacherous stretch of highway that most of us use daily for work.

On July Fourth, the town hosts a giant fireworks display. It used to be primarily for locals, but now it's been discovered: people from Dayton, Mark Twain, Carson City, and beyond start arriving at dusk. Parked on people's driveways, streets, vacant lots, you name it—they set up camp and begin to feast. There are only three roads in and out of Virginia City, and at firework's end, the entire town comes to a halt. We have stopped driving to our friends to watch the spectacle. It is easier to walk to the end of the street. For one night, every reserve sheriff must come out and play traffic cop. Inevitably, the lone drunk finds the sidewalk and proceeds to make his Rambler fit. Somehow the town doesn't burn down, and most of the tourists get home. None of us are ever sure of its efficacy—inviting thousands to watch the night sky on a usually dry and windy evening, but it goes on. We are assured we need the tourists for business, which is like being assured we need the rattlers to keep the rabbit population down.

No mother in her right mind would want to stand in the dust and smoke and howl of two-cycle engines for the weekend named in her honor, but until recently, the motorcycle races were held on Mother's Day. How that agreement finally came to pass is best left unknown because I think mothers, in retrospect, got shafted and would not agree to such terms today. The town has always seemed like a playground to people and usually that's OK. But when the wild events are over we go on with our lives. I used to ride motorcycles and loved doing it, but the proximity to our daily lives makes it hard to have a normal life. Perhaps that is why we have six months of snow—it is quiet and relatively peaceful, which makes living here exceptional. All of us have different ideas about the love-hate relationship with tourists. They bungle through our lives with happy questions, but the plain fact is we need them. The town almost died in the 1940s. Without some regular revenue stream it will die again. It's finding the right balance of cultural and gaudy tourism—something we work on to this day. Everybody wants to live in that perfect place, but this place is rough-hewn and has a long history of exploitation. Changing those norms is difficult. One of the best things that has happened has been the restoration of the cemetery, which almost every tourist runs to the minute they park their car. The Comstock Cemetery Foundation has painted and repaired the fences, made a booklet describing the cemetery, done extensive restoration of the facility, and made it worth visiting.

The preservation centerpiece is the Fourth Ward School Museum, a four-story building that housed 880 students with a gymnasium on the fourth floor in its heyday. Until a decade ago, some of its former pupils ran the Crystal Bar. Bill and Margaret Marks were precisely the kind of people tourists came to see: someone who knew about the history of the town, someone who could tell them what it was like to live here during the last century. Historic preservation is a big deal on the Comstock—with Piper's Opera House, St. Mary's Art Center, the Firemen's Museum, and a host of other sites, it is the backbone of what people want when they come: a meaningful experience. Much of this preservation has happened in the last two decades. It has literally been life-saving for the town. It's the balance of "stepping back in time" and stepping into a future we desire that is critical.

For now, we just blink and laugh—because the tourists trump all practical knowledge. When they walk down our street, a dead end, and ask how to get to the train, we point to the last three signs by which they walked. When they can't find a restroom, we tell them which places will let tourists in if it's winter, and where the lone public restroom is in summer. When they need food, we give them the names of the eateries on C Street, and hope they find one of them. I like talking to visitors from other countries because most of them think this is such an unusual physical place, like Park City, but on the edge of a mountain. They have learned something about it and want to see its remains—a mineshaft, a remnant of period clothing, the cookware, and the houses that might live on. Some just need directions. My neighbor has painted beautiful signs on most of the street corners—all this to help with navigation. The train, for all its smoky presence, has gone a long way to restoring the image of another era to the community. When it arrives I see real pleasure in the faces of the visitors. It makes this place a destination to go *to*—and we must complete that expectation. We must find a tourism commerce that will keep the community alive and satisfy its one million visitors per year.

It is hard to know what that answer is—particularly in the 21st century. As one who has lived here some time, there is a further balance that must be struck: challenging the idea of what tourism might mean. What if tourism made it possible for the merchants to survive the long winter? What if it was something that drew people to consider the cultural history of the place? What if it changed the business landscape to be sustainable? What new tourists would come, what businesses would need to be here, what changes would we, the residents, need to make, to bring Virginia City into this new era of embracing a vital present day?

*   *   *

Despite the weather and the mountain, there has been steady commerce on the Comstock. When we first arrived in 1980, there was a grocery store with a butcher shop. Denis Pecoraro made fresh sandwiches, talked long with every visitor and saw to it the town was properly represented to locals and visitors alike.

Uncle Pat and Mutley, his obese dog, ran a similar store for many years after Denis closed and served as part-time banker to his patrons on credit. He took great pleasure in edifying the visitor's with a local's perspective.

Gordon Lane ran the Union Brewery, told ribald stories and kept up the appearance of the town ne'er-do-well.

The Hungry Miner, in the former location of the Sun Mountain Artworks Gallery, was the quintessential breakfast place and its proprietors made absolutely divine pies, like pumpkin praline. Sometimes we woke them up late at night, craving a peanut butter pecan pie, and the baker and her husband staggered to the door to meet us, pie in hand, until the IRS caught up with them and suddenly it went dark.

Lynn Leong ran the Sharon House, a fine Chinese restaurant for nearly thirty years. We had our wedding rehearsal dinner there, but when he retired, it closed.

In the late '90s, Walden's Coffee House opened and we thought we'd died and gone to Berkeley. The Comstock Arts Council held poetry readings and concerts there. It was a happening place until the proprietors pulled out: not enough revenue.

Debby and I dream often of finding such a place tomorrow and just then, it arrives. Now we have the Roasting House coffee house and we pray it will last through the telltale winters and into the future of this community.

After the Union Brewery closed, we gave up hope of finding real beer but if you want a beer with a view, go to the Bucket of Blood.

Pascal's run a haberdashery for fifteen years. He ships his hats all over the world and has a six-week backlog. How rare in this time of machine-made things to see a craft like his return to sustain a community. If I had to say what the key to local commerce is, this would be it: love of craft, like my neighbor who ran a western Americana bookstore. Love alone cannot sustain an enterprise, but all of these businesses contribute to our quality of life.

When I think of entrepreneurs, Jeff and Paul come to mind. They have run several high-quality antique and mercantile stores— kept the lights on for decades in buildings that would have been dark. Most recently, they opened the Cobb Mansion, a bed and breakfast that does so well it needs no advertising.

There have been many more small merchants who made a difference—a boutique dress store, a children's toy store—mostly handmade, a mineral and gem store, and an Indian art store. The place that gave us the most comfort was Merle and Michele Koch's Silver Stope, a jazz club and restaurant. The interior looked like a mineshaft with Koch's piano at the back. He played for many years in New Orleans and knew countless musicians that he hosted in his club. The walls were filled with black and white stills of Dixieland jazzmen like Pete Fountain. An uncanny idea, but it took and ran until 1986 when he succumbed to throat cancer. We longed for the club to return when it closed. We had jazz at our fingertips. Jazz in the middle of winter when the streets were filled with snow and we walked to the club, ate slow as the music began. Jazzmen went out of their way to stop at the Stope and because of its reputation, Koch had an audience, snow or not.

When I walked into the Stope, it made me feel relaxed and energized. I relinquished something of the day and settled into conversation. Jazz began to be a source of freedom, a rhythmic exhaling, and a potent antidote to the day's labor. Nothing could soothe or free me like jazz, the urgent satisfaction of that art form. Being a musician, he knew how valuable it was and wanted to share it—even in so small a place as Virginia City. Clubs come and go, but his did not. He watched jazz thrive in our community. It became a destination, a place tourists and locals sought out. A place of authenticity—something we desperately need today.

This wasn't the only musical institution on the Comstock. In the 1960s the Red Dog Saloon was the preeminent place for early rock and roll. The Charlatans, Big Brother, Dan Hicks, and many other bands played there. Debby's former student, Mary Works Covington, did a documentary on it that preserved its history and cultural significance to the San Francisco psychedelic music scene ("The Life and Times of the Red Dog Saloon"). Today, Loren and Sue Pursel have resurrected it from obscurity and Big Brother has returned to play three times sans Janis, but the stand-ins were nearly as bluesy as she. Like Walden's, they have partnered with many groups, including ours, to make musical tourism a staple of this community.

Few people see the economic vitality of tourism in its richest form. If it is not organic and central to the lives of its residents, a business will struggle. The Stope challenged those norms. No one imagined the club would succeed outside an urban area. Yet Koch's vision of an outlet for jazz trumped all expectations. This is what is most needed: commerce driven by passion, not greed. We need people who love what they make, do, share, create, explore, build, and serve. We need more Merle Kochs, people who see an opportunity others cannot and who will risk to bring it to life, *because they must.* It is the only way anything good gets done. Miles never went to Spain but he *had* to make an album about it, and it is close to Spain in mood, temperament, and style. Koch had to make a jazz club, not an imitation with recorded tracks, but the improvisation of four people working from a fixed melody. This is innovation, what succors the dream of success.

Our work in this community is no different. At first, we were frequently alone, trying to find the precise element of commerce that would enable us to succeed. But we did so out of passion. We did not sell things; we offered a possible future, one that was informed by many hands: health care, counseling, youth and early childhood programs, and violence-free communities. None of this was sexy but it was love and risk that made the work possible, and like the Stope, part of the greater whole. It was jazz of the everyday, caring at its most primary level.

Our work provides a foundation from which a healthy community can be built. It is not a bar, a restaurant, or a gift store but it is a place of very real social commerce, where people of all walks of life come to connect with others. A community's fabric is created at this level; concern is not a commodity. It must be developed. This is what we *do*. Like the poet Kenneth Patchen said, "Caring is the only daring, oh you know it."

CHAPTER TWENTY-SIX

Dressing for Fire

In the summer when we lie down to sleep, all of the windows are open. There is stillness in the house. Sometimes we hear a whippoorwill, an owl, or the crazed howl of the coyote. It is only when they stop that sleep comes. Occasionally, if a new bird strays from its migratory path, it startles us from sleep. We sleep soundly, deeply, most nights, but when Debby pushes on my arm I know why: smoke has come into the room like an unwanted bird that has strayed from its path. I turn and look north from the bed—is the red shadow on the mountains facing Reno? I walk to the bathroom: is it coming from the west, from Tahoe, or is it further south in the Pine Nuts or Carson Valley? This smoke is a terrible smell. No one who lives here has escaped its reach. It is so dry in summer that fire becomes an element of dread: it can swallow a block of homes in minutes. In 2012, two different wind-caused fires in south Reno consumed thirty homes each in a matter of hours. We lie back down and hope it is not close, but hope also, it is not near the houses of friends because too many have lost everything.

I was driving home from the prison when flames consumed Carson City. All of the hills on its west side had burned or were burning. The city was filled with smoke. I couldn't see the Capital dome less than a mile from my car, and I knew the smoke would scar the most vulnerable: pets, children, and grandparents. That fire burned for days before they could put it out. Often it is caused by wind but sometimes it is a stupid mistake—ash from a barbeque, a spark from a chainsaw, even a controlled burn by the forest service.

When I drove up Paradise View on the hills above Carson, Art and his wife were there. Our good friends were standing in the rubble—their home had vanished. They had done all the right things—concrete tile roof, cleared the sage and brush to the property edge, and still flame arced from pine tree to pine tree. A spark started his siding on fire and it was over. The hardest part was that homes fifty yards away were still standing. The flame hopscotched from one home to another but in no particular order. It was so hot the fireman could not get their trucks close enough to fight it. There was nothing any of us could say. Our friends had saved their photos, computer, and dog, but the rest was gone—instantly. Some dervish of heat had torn their lives in half.

Caprice blew down that canyon. Caprice opened a house to fire and left. Left our friends and their neighbors searching for what to do: rebuild, relocate, or leave? The insurance adjusters look good on TV; in person it's not quite so pretty. We were lying on the beach at Camp Richardson on Tahoe's south shore in 2007 with our friends from Southern California. Debby worked with the woman when she was a counseling intern at Cal State Fullerton. The lake was calm—we were talking, enjoying the summer heat. I turned over to look up and thought it was a cloud but it kept getting darker, bigger, and there was no wind. It grew to the size of a football field in twenty minutes. There was something wrong—it was not a thundercloud. It was fire. "We need to leave now," I said. One hour later they closed Highway 89, the primary north/south artery on the west shore of the lake. By the time we got to the hotel at Stateline—less than seven miles from where we were—one-inch flakes of ash were falling on my car. To the west, where the fire was burning it looked like an oil field had exploded—it was completely out of control. The hardest part about a forest fire is that it makes its own weather. It creates firestorms so it must be fought from the air and the ground, if it can be fought. The

Angora Fire burned more than 250 homes. A smoldering campfire started it and one of those homes belonged to friends. Again, the house across the street was fine; theirs was leveled to the ground. He was a teacher, she worked with people with disabilities. They and their girls lived in an apartment for a year. Their home is rebuilt but it took two years to settle with the insurance company.

Fire does not ask why. Smoke floats in the room and touches everything. I have lived with that smell through thirty winters. I try to be cautious—I never let the stove get too hot or leave it unattended. And yet, it provides: we heated our old house exclusively with wood and since moving across the street, I light the stove almost every winter morning. I installed this stove because a fire calms me. Ben Wesner's son sold me this stove—it is old now, the firebricks are breaking inside. Last year, the chimney sweep bent the flu plate so it is harder to balance in the open position. Cutting and stacking wood gives me more pleasure than I can say. The last thing I do before leaving is cut kindling for Debby. I smoke salmon over a wood fire year round and in the summer, fashion a makeshift barbeque of bricks in the driveway. Leandro, our student from Buenos Aires, taught me to cook ribs slowly over hard wood coals. It took hours—if you could touch the grill the heat was just right. This meant lighting a fire when the cheat grass and the cornflowers had died, when the yard was brown. I hosed the ground for thirty feet and kept a bucket of water close by.

On the Fourth of July, Debby and I walk to the end of our block and set up chairs. For years it has been the one time when we see all of our neighbors. The wind is usually howling and the last moisture has disappeared from the Comstock. By the time the show starts we are under blankets—cold, nervous, and excited. Each year we take bets: what locust tree will start on fire, what scraggly sage will burst into flame, what spark will ignite the grass? It is an anomaly of living in this high desert town. Even though fire is what consumes the landscape, they stage one of the best firework displays in northern Nevada. The entire fire department lies in wait: trucks, water buffaloes, jeeps, fire engines, command posts, and more to keep the town from burning down. To their credit they do. They have done so repeatedly. When real fire comes to the Comstock, their response is quick and professional.

Twice since we have lived here fire has threatened Virginia City. From my front yard I watched the tankers drop the red borax retardant on the hills, maybe a mile from town. A single-engine aircraft led the DC-3 tankers through the smoke and into the ravines too steep to fight on foot. This aerial support is called in for fires such as these. When those planes come to this little town we all worry. Another time, at work, the fire came within a half mile of our office. We started to load the most important files in the car and hoped that the tankers and the ground crew could hold the perimeter. Our building, as I said, was one of three to withstand the 1870s fire. It is restored now but we could never replace it. Fire destroys. I just wanted it to stop, to move away from the buildings on the south end of town. The wind was erratic and all it took was one small ember. Our roof was still shingles that were over forty years old. They would have ignited in minutes. I watched until the dark came and the fire blew farther south. I went home, ate dinner and hoped the phone did not ring. Smoke was everywhere and it had come into the room with noise, sirens, and fear.

Strangely, this draws a community together—no one is exempt. A fireman has taken me from my home on a backboard after I rolled my truck on Geiger Grade. I pulled a snowplow driver from his cab when he rolled his truck. You depend on one another; you do what is necessary to save, to protect, to serve. This is the best part of a small community—in a crisis people pitch in. I imagine the same could be said of a city block—but here we have no choice. If my neighbor's home burns, the consequences are felt throughout the community. This has happened more than once—and it is never good. The woman who stands before you has a child, a suitcase, and dress—the nylon dripping from the hanger. The teacher who lives in a trailer for four months while they gut his house is not any teacher—he sold us our house. The grandfather who hunts must wait out the season with his adult children while the contractor rushes to beat the snow. When the fire burns so close to your house you can see the flame, you immediately feel nauseous—it has shredded someone's life. You know them, talk to them in the post office. You know the men and women standing on the ladder trying to put it out. You know the people who live on either side of the flames. You know what this place has been: many artists lived in this home—painters, poets, novelists, and musicians. It was from the 1870s, almost historic in the Intermountain West, and now it is an idea. A friend is battling the banks, the insurance company, and more because he was the caretaker. It is never easy to reconstruct a life, to move on after such devastation. It is an act of will that is further complicated by caprice—why me and not them? Why this home and not that home? Why did it visit my room?

*   *   *

And yet: I ask my friend with a backhoe to come to my yard. I want him to dig a pit to roast a pig. I have no idea how to do it but I want to and so I read and ask and practice: surely this can be learned. My friend asks how deep. I imagine six feet. In Jarbidge, in northeastern Nevada, they have dug a hole in the ground and lined it with steel for an annual barbeque. That mountain town of forty year-round residents, the site of the last stagecoach robbery in America, lights a bonfire of soft wood and then hard and it smolders to coals. They throw in rocks and when they are heated, they move them to the coals at the edge of the pit. They wrap the meat in burlap, put a piece of sheet metal over the coals, another on top of the meat, and return the hot rocks and coals—what amounts to a Dutch oven beneath the ground. They cap it with a final plate of steel and let it cook for twenty-four hours. There is nothing to compare with slow-cooked meat. The whole town gathers to celebrate the passage of Independence Day. A tradition that has been going on for decades despite the fact that Jarbidge almost burned down more than once. The most recent forest fire in 2008 spread for miles and burned out of control in the Humboldt National Forest for over two weeks. The geography was overwhelming and the cost to fight it prohibitive. They let it burn out, but kept watch on the town.

Twice we have dug a pit barbeque in our backyard. The first time was beginner's luck: I spent the day gathering sage to start the fire, juniper and mountain mahogany to sustain it, and then borrowed oak and almond from friends. I did not know how deep to make the coals and so guessed: at least six inches below and four above. I asked four friends to help, hoping that our two garden hoses and buckets of water would keep the sparks at a minimum. It was September, dry and dusty. Thankfully, there was no wind. Had there been wind, we could not have done it. The flames were over ten feet, almost to the top of the roof. I knew they would subside, but I did not want them to spread. We squirted every spark, every sudden jump of flame and slowly, the heat began to rise in waves. It took more than an hour to build enough coals to last through the night. I went in the house and brought the pig from the bathtub. It had been sitting on ice overnight. When I carried it up the stairs the day before, my mother-in-law asked if I had a body in the clear plastic bag. No, it's just a pig I told her, but she had her doubts. My mother-in-law was game for just about anything but this tested her religion: she thought her son-in-law had gone off the rails. I assured her it would be wonderful and she rolled her eyes as if I had no idea what wonderful was. I loved that woman, think of her every day, and miss her like Debby does but probably not as much. When we were in Sacramento to visit Debby's sister, Winni ran into my room: "Mom's in cardiac arrest. Get in the car." I ran into the hospital barefoot, still not sure what had happened or why. She had had a heart attack but was supposed to recover. She would be home in a week and I could pilfer cookies from her jar. When I got to her bed she grabbed my face and kissed my lips hard. I held her and then walked to the waiting area. Her heart literally tore in half. I think she had too much pain, too much sorrow, trying to take care of her husband. This was a woman who was in the underground at 16, ferrying messages to and from the allied pilots shot down in her Belgian village of Heers. This was a woman who lied to German soldiers so that the pilots could live. One of them was her husband. One of them flew multiple missions behind enemy lines. One of them kept the B-17 in the air, burning, until the last man parachuted out. One of them kept it flying twice, on fire, to save his buddies. He was in the waiting room with us hoping this was not the end.

When I used to cut wood for Gladys, she stood outside in sweltering heat and held the ladder. The chainsaw was over my head, my goggles were fogged with sweat. "Be careful, don't get hurt," and then her words faded when I set the blade into the wood. Tall scraggly junipers, they kept dancing when I touched them with the chainsaw. They fell all over the driveway and I tried to push them from the roof. Bob came outside, lit a cigarette, and thanked me. I watched them for over two decades, braiding the fine language of marriage.

I knew Gladys was joking when she laughed at me from the couch. I knew she would love the pig. No one liked to eat more than she. Those years of living in darkness, on root vegetables when the Germans stalked her village, with a Jewish orphan in the house, those infinite years when the Allies were farther away than the moon, gave her patience and perspective. She was frugal—I teased her unmercifully about the coupons. At the store the cashiers would run when she came in. She was the only woman who left the grocery store with more money than she brought in. I didn't know about hunger when I met Gladys, but she would teach me. Her diary of the pilots, elaborate drawings of their faces and flight jackets, read like a telegram from an underground museum. Gladys loved that pig. Winni cut it up in minutes. She was a physician. My good friend threw the pieces on the Weber for a final searing and even the vegetarians went off the wagon for the afternoon. This is what fire brought us. This is how we gathered to share food. This is one thing I could give to Gladys.

*   *   *

Do you stop living because the air is filled with fear? This is what I asked Fadhil Al-Azzawi, the Iraqi poet when he came to Nevada in 2007. For three weeks we drove up and down the state as he read his poems in universities, libraries, and bookstores. At one point we were driving around the west shore of Lake Tahoe on the same road that had been closed to fire that summer's day. It was March and the road was snowy. We listened to the radio in the silence. It was at the height of the Iraq War. A pediatrician was being interviewed live from Baghdad. The journalist asked, "How can you go on delivering babies when the war will take them from your hands?" Fadhil laughed because he knew the answer. The doctor spoke immediately: "We have endured warfare for centuries. We must go on. There is nothing permanent. We cannot stop living until the war is over."

She continued: "Do you have children?"

"Yes, four, and we may have another one."

"*Now*," she asked incredulously, "when Baghdad is so unstable?"

"Yes. Is it any worse for the refugees of a dozen countries? They have not stopped living, they have not waited for the dictator to leave."

Fadhil leaned forward: "We are not fatalists but we keep on. We have for centuries. If we waited for peace we would have died out long before the British came." Fadhil was tortured for four years, a political prisoner before he fled his homeland. He has not seen one family member since. They communicate through messengers. His house is a home for squatters. He has lived in Berlin since leaving Iraq. He and his wife are writers. His poems and novels poke fun at the idea of permanence, the notion that you could live just as you wanted. In the face of extremes, he laughs to keep perspective just like my late mother-in-law. It's not death they are afraid of; it's living without the chance to go on that they fear.

*   *   *

Somewhere then, the smoke takes its place. We will live each day until the next Fourth of July. We will gather our chairs, walk to the end of the street and see our neighbors again. We will tell lies about the fireworks and secretly hope that a locust catches on fire. In the cold, unnerving wind, we will walk back to our homes. An ember will smolder, but just as surely, dawn will come and something will appear—a blue flower in the myrtle, a bird at the window. There will be a mark of renewal. We will make our way forward, just as the first miners in this clapboard town did. The fire and the wind will exact something from us, but we will wake after the smoke comes in the room.

My wife turns in bed. I look into the night sky. This is how we dress for fire.

CHAPTER TWENTY-SEVEN

Losing the Library

When a library closes, some part of the town closes, too, its breath taken from the room of ideas.

In 2012, our library closed, the result of budget cuts. This cut to public access to information was met with an unsettling mix of outrage and apathy. Some felt it needed to be shuttered long ago, a waste of taxpayer dollars. Others, like Debby, who happened to be sitting in the last library board meeting at the time, said it was "unequivocally wrong," which led to the immediate discharge of the collection, some 18,000 volumes, to Community Chest who herewith, became the steward of the collection. We didn't ask for it, but when the board took action to pass it on to Community Chest, it was an act of faith and trust, born of years of perseverance. This is how things change when the breath goes out of the room: we could serve as the library's bridge to the future.

A library is not something she or I knew how to run. No part of our graduate training extolled the virtue of maintaining a public forum for books. But all of me knew, like Debby, this was wrong. This led to more things we did not know: how to store about ten tons of books? I called Squeek LaVake, the pianist, who had an empty warehouse on a slab. Ever the willing neighbor, she agreed to let us store the collection in her building for an unknown period of time. Then we waited and wondered: how do we construct a library with no building?

The only person who might have an answer was my good friend and former Washoe County Library director, Nancy Cummings. Very soon, she mobilized fifteen volunteer librarians to thin the collection to 12,000 volumes. The rest were returned to the high school for possible use at its former site. More than a year passed— still no building. Again, we enlisted Nancy and her colleague's help to start a children's library in the limited space we had upstairs in the community center. The weight of the entire collection prohibited us from placing it in that space, but it could support 200 books for children. She ordered colorful boxes and rugs to make it a welcoming place and shortly thereafter, in 2013, the children's library opened.

During this time there was much discussion about Community Chest's mission. Were books, lots of books, in our mission? No, they were not. But literacy, well-being, and public access to information were a significant part of our programs. We ran academic remediation programs for high school youth and pre-K educational programs on five buses. We were no stranger to literacy and its importance. You cannot do community building work and exempt some things from examination and include others. This library was part of the community for twenty-three years, started by the venerable Lucy Bouldin. My boys and I spent countless Saturday mornings with her in the "old" library at the high school. My late friend and I ran poetry programs in the library and over time, Lucy built a strong collection of poetry and Nevada history. Lucy was a lighthouse for the young people and the public. She was also one of the few black women in town. A gifted singer, former music teacher, and literary champion, the library's closure was a direct blow to her. This upset many people as I said, and an equal number did not know or care about her demise. The greater sadness was the emptiness left by her retirement amidst the chaos of dismantling the library.

Shuttering the library was not an option. I pleaded with the county to restore minimal funding, which they did. They, too, had been hurt in this process and it would take time to heal the rift.

The county was in the middle of a recession and it was a logical place to cut the budget. Before long, it grew into a conflagration until sides were taken and it closed. One thing Debby and I have learned is to make peace in these difficult situations, try to find the common ground in what was a hornet's nest. To do otherwise would signal failure for all of us. Books are the cornerstone of an educated citizenry. Knowledge is what usually keeps us from the arcane warfare of the past. We can choose to understand the other's perspective. It is in books we explore other frames of reference, other models of being. Ours was not a choice of board, staff, or funding, but of how we would live as a community. Books and their houses, the libraries of this globe, have been essential places of discovery for centuries. Long before the Internet, they were the equalizer. The mind had no authority save what was learned— witness all times of intellectual growth in history. But still, how does one build a library on such shaky ground?

Books are a prism to another world. From my teaching at the prison I knew they were lifesaving. Knowledge, indeed poetry, became the one thing the men could rely on to lead them out of incarceration. This is not new; many colleges have prison programs and the judicial system has long conceded the importance of education to reducing recidivism. But it was more than that: books were my small room of concentration. For years I never let go of a book I read—it was a marker of becoming educated. I read everything to Nevada and Cody, hoping they, too, would become readers. I listened as great writers took me with them on long journeys from home. I fell in love with Steinbeck before I fell in love with Debby. Both have set me free, and poetry, for all its malcontents, has literally been the one activity that has sustained me—just as it has for the 100-plus men in the workshop. When you have nothing, poetry becomes liberating. It is the foundation on which you begin to reshape consciousness. It is the way out of the darkness, often of our own creation. The ancients knew this: Tu Fu and Li Po wandered, rife with personal suffering, but they nevertheless saw joy in every egret, leaf, or cup of wine. They saw the human mind transported by the mosaic of this art form. It freed them of momentary struggle as it has freed readers and poets alike for generations. To close a library would be to close a mind. It simply couldn't be done. We must not tempt ignorance.

In the summer of 2014, we received word the medical clinic was pulling out of the community center, an equal sadness after so many years of effort to start it. But it was on the first floor and on a slab. We could move the collection into the building, free up Squeek's warehouse, and open it to the public once again. With the county's help we were able to hire a librarian and before long, offer services throughout the county. Nancy and her team continued to be vigilant supporters as we nursed the fledgling operation back to health. Again, with the constant support of volunteers, community, and our team, it slowly became vital in its new location. It also became a model for how information could be integrated with mental health, youth, and family services—a health and wellness hub.

We live in a time when the printed word is under siege. Publishing, as we know it, has become instantly available and accessible. Both trends have made the written word and the craft of publishing them an anachronism. Books will not go away any more than soap or light or spring, but just as libraries all across the country shrink in size and import, and struggle to find their place in the 21st century, we must never let the slow dissolution of the public house for books become the norm. I remember reading, as a teenager, the story of the camps in a weekend. Nothing could shut out its message. But I also remember sitting next to a man on a plane who bragged about *never* having read a book. It gave birth to this stanza from the poem "The Unread Books":

> …My death
> will be the voices
> of librarians
> chanting the names
> of the unread books.

There is a place for electronic and printed media. It is not an either/or situation. It is an opportunity to use both media to express our best thinking. Story is the breath we pass from generation to generation. It is how we measure our presence in the world, however fragile. Story transforms the molecules of existence into meaning. It is meaning I choose, whatever the consequence. Just as Gutenberg saw the printing press as liberating, all forms of media now compete for our attention. Are they liberating? Who knows? What I hope for is a breadth of expression, printed and electronic, that refuses easy solutions like closing a library when funding runs out. The library is the most public of institutions. Like school, it is the entrée to full participation in society. Without it, we turn away from the very thing that literature has left us— the solace of the written word. I am grateful to have lived in the comfort of that solace and hope to do so in the days ahead, as I can now return to our library.

CHAPTER TWENTY-EIGHT

Waiting in the Dental Line

It is April 2012, the month of many names—Eliot's month of "The Wasteland," the tax man's month, and the month when spring returns to winter over and over on the Comstock. It is the morning of daffodils lying flat, their yellow flowers pinched to the andesite terrace in front of the house. I think they will never survive. This is the third day of their falling to freezing temperatures. How can anything live in this climate? How, indeed?

I drive down Six Mile Canyon, east into the clouds and snow of morning. An ordinary dawn except the desert peach has started to bloom, and then I know that despite the cold and unrelenting wind spring will return. Spring will come back just as it has a hundred times before. More signs of life: there are horses at the road edge, and further east, a lone horse tries to find grass in the sage. Highway 50 spreads to the horizon and in the distance some shimmer of water at Lake Lahontan. There are new buildings here—schools in Silver Springs, the places of promise and hope in any community. Today, hundreds of people will come to this high school with the hope of being seen for their medical and dental concerns. Today, an equal number of volunteers will try to serve them. The irony is that so few will hear this conversation. In our political climate, few will branch out to disappear among those who need more than trivial conversation to assuage their pain. Few will recognize this face in line that has but one thing to hold: the hope of being treated.

Two women sit at the dental table with me. They have volunteered most of their adult lives. They have stood in these lines. Their own teeth need dental work. They have children, some of whom are now adults and are also in these lines. They have made a pact with the future: if I give of my time, perhaps their world will have what mine did not. It is the second day of listening to stories: I am asked to translate what any boy could translate with hand signals: my mouth hurts, my tooth is broken, my face is swollen. I ask repeatedly, what is it you *need*—fillings, extractions, cleaning? Some cannot reply, some only want to be in the line, to be anonymous without a reason. Some cannot open their mouths. They fear what lies inside. They fear I will judge them, and yet those who accompany them ask us to look, to verify, to string the loss of dignity to the next chair where they will wait to be seen. What I cannot say is that one-fifth will not find the magic hands of a dentist. What I cannot say is that you will be turned away.

Another volunteer has come to the table both days. She has a tooth that is loose and it is about to fall out. She has just taken a job as a receptionist. She is worried she will lose the job if she cannot smile. She has no other resources. She has no one to ask for help. This is the anomaly we call health care. My dear friend and activist Christy McGill organized this event. She did this because the lines continued to form even as they remained invisible to those who could intercede on their behalf. One state legislator, one Congressional representative, and two county commissioners are here. They will return with something of the day on their hands. They will sit before dais after dais and try to explain the conundrum of poverty. They will work for an economy that will permit more than piecemeal legislation. They will return to their constituents with some reminder of living outside the community. They will not, however, stand by the people in this line because it is hardest to be without recourse. I tried to imagine any one of the individuals in this line in a relationship, loving someone, caring for others, waking to a mirror that would not intercede on their behalf, going to work, hiding in a cubicle, or dressing for out of doors year-round so that their faces could be covered.

*　　　　*　　　　*

This is the first year of the Medical Outreach Response Event (MORE). Christy and her team have been here since dawn. There are lines to each station—glasses, medical, dental, mental health, and other resources. We are in a high school gymnasium. Every volunteer has a purpose and they try, in their own way, to render assistance. By mid-morning, it becomes clear that many people in the dental line will not get seen. They will go home much as they came—with the pain of tooth decay.

Around the corner, in the library, the volunteers offer blood pressure checks and basic physical health screenings. Off the hallway, Erik and other colleagues provide counseling, which today might mean counseling on how to cope with the lack of health care. I get up from my station and walk back to the waiting line for the dental van: have there been any changes, is there space for one more person to be seen?

The van is a long mobile home that has been outfitted for portable dental care. Inside, a dentist and three hygienists quickly assess what is required for each patient: fillings, extractions, sealants, and more. Miraculously, they keep their sense of humor about them and most of the children exit the van with smiles. Some adults have as many as four extractions. Their mouths are swollen but they are grateful.

At the other end of the gymnasium are the yellow jackets of the Lion's Club. They are distributing glasses to the people at their station. There are dozens of volunteers from the local clubs.

In the bleachers, families wait with the children. The kids try to play on the wooden seats. It is too cold to go outside, and yet the smokers cough in the wind. Christy's associates run from station to station with a walky-talky in their hands. They are in charge of seeing that every patient stop is adequately staffed and they have the resources they need.

Beyond the gym, the volunteers huddle over sandwiches and coffee in the student cafeteria. The morning has the feel of a highly organized Red Cross outpost except that there is no perceived emergency here. That is the paradox: except for the 500-plus people who have come for services, the need for medical and dental treatment is unknown. Were it not for their faces, it would remain so. But Christy and her team have seen these faces too often and they resolved to do something about it.

In two years she will bring the group of medical volunteers, Remote Area Medical, or RAM, to coordinate the event. It will have grown to be staged in Reno and Las Vegas. In the interim, she lobbied the legislature to enable volunteer medical personnel to come from other states to provide services in Nevada. In a word, she could not forget their faces. RAM has coordinated events like these all over the world and so, after months of planning and preparation, when they arrive in Nevada, the treatment is highly coordinated and effective. It runs as efficiently as an assembly line.

Still, I want to follow the people out the door, into the wind of Silver Springs. I want to know the person they left behind today, what they cannot tell us on their medical intake sheets. I want to know who it is that told them this is all there is, and how it became truth.

In an irony I couldn't make up, I returned to the high school to teach poetry in the gifted and talented class last fall. I had a great morning with eight juniors and seniors. Their teacher was one of the most exciting English teachers I had met. I thought this is how school should be for all kids—enchanted and challenging. When I walked to my car I remembered that volunteers—many who were at the MORE event—were distributing food one hundred yards from the high school. I looked at the line: old women with oxygen tanks, infants in the arms of young people and everyone in between. Some of the young people were just a year out of high school and yet this was their future—a line to something almost free in the cold wind and dust of the desert. How is it the brightest and the hungriest can be separated by a hundred yards? What perverse angel led them to these places? Some part of me did not want to know and I slipped away, just like them, before I could find out.

*   *   *

Back at the dental table, I grabbed a coffee and resumed taking names. A young girl asked me if her stuffed animal, a cat, could get a new tooth. It was almost funny, almost like relief. But what surrounded her—the stigma of being poor—also waited in the dental line. It was alone, off to the edge of the line, and occasionally it moved closer to the table. It moved closer to us. We could not see it, could not find its name or number in the lottery. We drew tickets from the five-pound coffee can and hoped it would not come forward, hoped it would stay in the background, hoped it would be calm in the unrelenting queue. But each hour it made itself known: "Show him your teeth, *show him*," and she could not until finally, in desperation, she did so. I stared across the gym floor and wished for some miracle of transformation, some induction scene that would replace what we could not. This is the irony that also waited in line: in a minute, these people could be treated. In an emergency, these people would be treated. In almost any other situation, there would be an expectation of common sense response. If you cannot eat, smile, or kiss without pain, how can you work, attend school, and participate in the normal affairs of family, peers, and community?

What is it we want from one another as people? What is it we need to belong? The first thing, it seems to me, is dignity. We need to know that our lives are not in vain. We need to know that if we must endure the indignity of poor health, we are valued. The line most needed, the line to find compassion, is the line that remains. Thankfully, that was the one thing that could be given freely. That was the most artful moment of the weekend—people's undying concern for one another. But in this world, this world that is broken into two—those with access and those without—it will take more than compassion to break this cycle of poverty. It will take leaders with guts and vision to marshal the resources to steer this globe to equity, to justice. I know those terms are tired. They are as tired as the people waiting in the dental line. They have been used over and over to ill effect and now they are lying in the room like used toys. They have no meaning of their own. They are disinterested playthings. They are tokens of civility.

It will take action. It will take you and me and the hundreds in that line to form a "more perfect union" of haves and have-nots. It is fine to be chaste with resources, with the implements of society so long as the resources provide for one's own. This is an old conversation; what troubles me is that we're still having it. I have heard people who know better surrender: we will always have poverty. People quote the Bible to demonstrate its existence, but the death of poverty may be the very thing that saves us. It may be the very thing that keeps us from killing one another when so little is at stake. We have to gone to war over skin color, religion, boundaries, and yes, food or the lack of it. I wonder if we have gone to war in search of something other than victory, something far subtler, far more difficult to articulate, like human dignity. I can already hear the naysayers—"We have always fought for this," but I want a conflict of ideas without casualties, a way forward that permits us to live in relative harmony.

As long as a few people have the gold there will be a dental line. It really does come down to you and me: we have to wait with them. We have to call out poverty's name, remind the hundreds and hundreds who could not come for care that their lives are not in vain. Harder still, we have to stand in the other lines, the lines at the seat of power. We have to have the courage to open our mouths and speak when we are called on, and we have to say what is needed. No amount of whitewashing will change this. The world we live in is directly proportionate to what we put in it. Hardest of all, we have to risk the indifference of privilege, have to speak when it is not heard, have to say the vows of isolation. Until we have been humiliated by those very words, we can know nothing of human suffering, much less its resolution.

*   *   *

That the daffodil should stand in stark contrast to this day that began so cold is something of an enigma. And yet it does on this Sabbath, this day after the dental line. Three freezes, three long nights in the high desert, and yet today its stems and flowers have risen in the modest sun. This is the same high desert that I return to for tranquility, for peace in the midst of an unforgiving world. A part of me did not want to drive to Silver Springs for fear of what I would see, of what I would encounter. A part of me wanted to be left alone, wanted to spend the weekend working in the yard, writing or even that most luxurious of activities, painting a watercolor. A part of me was afraid that the desert finally would not protect me from its least-known inhabitants. A part of me wanted to be removed from the killing freeze that brought the daffodils down. A part of me wanted to drive on, past Silver Springs, to Fallon, the birds of Stillwater, to the wildlife that skirts the road edge. And yet I could not choose indifference, could not veer to the left. The desert is my refuge, as are its people. This work will not be completed in my lifetime but I continue to hold out hope that we will find a way to bridge differences, which in the end may save us. I continue to hold out hope that the desert will be a place of refuge for all of us, not just those that thrive in its arid stillness.

I believe it was in the movie *City of Joy*, set in the former Calcutta, where the protagonist said the most important things—love, sex, and children—are shared without regard to riches. Hardly a hope, but a near-certainty nonetheless. Like the woman in that movie, maybe there is a woman in Silver Springs harboring the memory of her husband's secret need. Maybe she is lying next to him in the pale moonlight, hoping for the day redemption will come to release them from the coda of the desert: live hardy like the daffodil. Live below the frost line. Live where what you need is close by. Live without supposition. Live in the proximity of water, of people who care enough to remember this through the dry season. Live by the side of the road, out of the way. Live where you might be noticed and you might disappear. Live as if there is no other way to live. Scavenger, pilgrim, reptile—we are all of these and we scavenge for truth and beauty.

CHAPTER TWENTY-NINE

The Tarantula Crossing at Devil's Gate

It is fall in Virginia City, the latent time of year, when what was momentarily green returns to brown, the color for which we have no true name save living in its midst. I drive down Greiner's Bend, a 15% grade that trucks and buses stall on, then onto Gold Hill, and the breadth of the canyon below. I come to Devil's Gate, two rock outcroppings that close the mouth of the canyon. There is just enough road to drive between them. Something black is on the highway, something small, but it moves, slow like a turtle, determined to get to the other side, determined to migrate before the coming winter. In over thirty years I can remember one or two falls when I did not see a tarantula cross the highway. It is a migration not fully understood, but necessary for survival. Most of the time they make it. Perhaps they are too slow, perhaps they move at an uncertain pace and so the tires of cars and trucks somehow avoid them. I cannot think of a more vulnerable place to be—splayed on the highway—with twenty minutes or more yet to cross the blacktop.

These rocks were here long before the first wagons brought wood and water to the Comstock. This canyon has been carved by something greater than us, and the tarantula was also part of that time. It is trying to return to the rocks of that time, the shelter that will protect it from the kill frost and the snow and the occasional creek that runs through Silver City. It is a metaphor for how slowly we move, how much time must pass for each of us to cross a threshold of seasons, a threshold of living in this place longer than a generation.

In this fall of 2013 the mine developers have employed men in white suits and mouthpieces to inspect the ground for mercury contamination. Like the tarantulas, I drive by them too. Unlike them, I can leave, but choose to stay. I choose to make this my home. I don't want to live with contamination of any kind. I will settle for the minimum compromise—if you must dig, do it out of sight and do not harm this ground, this water, this history. A small promise rarely kept. Then I remember how the tarantula has lived through all of this and it makes no difference: we will go on with or without the digging. What will save us is what saved the people in the dental line—human compassion, human dignity, the will to make something sacred in the face of detractors.

After all, it is a mountain I live on, a mountain indifferent to time, to us, to digging, and yes, even the tarantula that crosses the highway for safety. While I have looked to the tarantula for some indication of survival, the mountain will not ask us, will not include us in the discussion. In our short time here, Debby and I, our boys who are now men, the family of friends, of co-workers, and community, have chosen to create a place in which to live. We have chosen the orneriest rock I know—the mine tailings—on which to build houses, schools, churches, and the post office with its six black and white pictures of a snowbound main street. We are no different from people who make community everywhere. We thread the silence with our toil. Sometimes we are rewarded with real change— the community center that finally emerged from the mine tailings has a health and wellness hub (we found a new health care provider), a library, programs for young people, and families. Sometimes we are discouraged and the thought of remaining is a burden. But I have lived in places where going outside is difficult, where breathing is difficult, where eating is a struggle. I cannot return to those places. Like my neighbors, I choose the indifference of this mountain.

Since I started working on this story that I was in such a hurry to write, this story that took thirty years to live, I have lost two of my neighbors and a third has moved away. The son of my neighbor who went to the end of street with us for twenty-four firework displays succumbed to the ravages of MD. Each of them was here for nearly the same amount of time—three decades—time we measure with our lives spent in relationship, in school, in work, in a *place*. I walked my dog last night and looked at their homes and realized when we moved here I had no knowledge of them, had no understanding of who lived behind the clapboard exteriors. I must have been a complete outsider to have not seen such history in their faces, but then I also realized it was only time in one place that could have given this knowledge of so many interwoven lives.

I remember those first years, typing early drafts on my trailer in the yard, the summer sun beating on my back, how happy I was to have discovered the silence of hundred-mile views, of ceramic beer bottles below my feet. When I built the deck for my pregnant wife, she laid in the sun like an hourglass of twin lives—hers and soon our son's. She was an answer to the confusion of my life; she let me know that I could continue on here, could make our home complete. Years later, when we returned from graduate school, I built a garage and wrote. I was never so happy. Those shingles that scratched my hands, my knees, those shingles that buried the wasps, those sweaty gloves I wore were messengers of labor, signals that I was alive. I took them to mean this is the pattern of your life. This is how you will go forward in this place: you and she will work for what you want, what you need. You will make it and in our persistence, made as many mistakes as not.

The slow road we took was filled with all that we lost. Our desire to create, not just poems but a livelihood that concentrated on people, on their well-being, meant we would stand in a hundred lines, meant we would go out at night and perch on the rocks at the edge of our driveway, numb with what desire had achieved. No one told us we couldn't build a community of people who cared, or live in a wilderness of wind and indifferent rocks. No one told me I couldn't shovel this earth, couldn't build a fence, and couldn't keep the rodents from killing our chickens. No one told me my house would bend in the wind, would succumb to the blades of dust, to the endless dissolution of wood. I'm grateful they didn't, grateful some chance of circumstance led me to one of my first students, Karen Wesner, who after class said, "You know, our friend just built a home in Virginia City and you may want to look at it," and I'm grateful she and her husband, Ben, have been the guardians of our time on this indifferent rock.

Even now I contemplate more building, more tearing down of the old house to make space for Debby and me, to create a room with a little more light, where we can sleep, where if the smoke comes in the window, we can shudder and stop, when in the smallest of hours, we lie together for want of time outside of time. I am grateful for the friends who made art possible in this place, who gave me a reason to write poetry when all I should have done is walk away. Thirty-plus years—it is not a lifetime but it is a time that we shared, it is a time that we moved slow, across something like a road, to safety, yes, but to the promise of what we could do together. In our stubborn refusal to turn back, we scored the trail with our momentary existence and perhaps came close to reaching the other side, the side of protection, and I would say harbor, but as you know, we have no water. We have only its outline, its remembrance on the desert below this mountain. All of this to get from here to there. It is not enough to define a story, not enough to explain a life's insistence, but we crossed, nonetheless.

CHAPTER THIRTY

Through the Saffron Light

It is the fourth time of passing through saffron light since starting on this journey of reflection. In the backyard the nectarine is red-orange, our time of leaf-fall. I have shut the sprinklers off and what's left of the grass has browned. Everything is burnished with a residue of things about to close. It is the season to prepare: stack the wood on the porch, split the kindling, and hide the garden tools in the shed.

This is where I began with those repetitive tasks that signal the approach of winter, and now I close with those same rituals: I must cut the oak and peach wood that I can't split with the axe. After many pulls, my tired Homelite chainsaw kicks to life and in the sawdust and sun I remember the years this saw gave in preparation for other winters. It was normal to cut and split two to three cords of piñon. Now I buy my wood, my time lost to other pursuits: keeping order at work so that I may write, and still, this labor that restores human faith—my so-called work—is no less dignified a record of my time in this place.

Since we started Community Chest, we have finished the first phase of the community center and are about to embark on the second. The first floor of the building is teeming with a health and wellness hub, a vibrant library, and the before- and after-school program for elementary youth. More youth programs share the upstairs, including a high school for at-risk youth. Over a hundred people a week access services in this building—something Debby and I dreamt of for nearly two decades.

This is how work gets done in a rural community: many hands embrace the bold idea of something larger for their future. When we began our work at Community Chest, we could not have imagined it would grow like it has. At our semi-annual retreat I told my colleagues we will probably have forty to fifty employees in the next ten years. How did this happen? How did we grow to become an agent of change? How did we raise millions of dollars to address the most obvious of human needs, and how is it we must address them still?

This morning I was at a fundraising breakfast for a homeless shelter in Reno. Friends and dignitaries were there—people who helped us build our facility. Several individuals spoke about their life-saving experiences in the shelter and how dignifying it was to take their voices back, particularly through a poetry workshop run by a volunteer English professor. I wished they had read from their poems, wished they had shared their experiences in that way.

I returned home to news for another person whose life had been touched by poetry: Cliff was granted parole. Cliff is one of a handful of men who have co-led the prison workshop. On a cold January morning he will step into this landscape and look for a friend, someone to be with on that first day of release. Debby and I will be in Costa Rica with Nevada and his wife, Brenna, for the holidays, but I will imagine how he looks at the Sierra Nevada without the apron of barbed wire, who he will touch or smell, what clothes he will wear, what shiver of recognition will permeate his spine when he encounters the first scent of being outside.

I wrote about reading Dylan Thomas in the workshop and tried to understand why I teach at the prison. In a word, it is this day that has finally come. I teach to betray the darkness, to return the gift of getting up in the freedom of one's room. So small these things, these inanimate things—a bed, a room, a job—and none of them tell the story of how long he has waited to experience their calm. Neither Cliff nor I knew if this day would come. Two years ago, when he was up for parole, his brother called to say he was driving up from Los Angeles to pick him up after he was released. I cautioned him: don't do it. It may not happen; it may never happen. He had to survive to find this day even if it did not exist in real time. His brother relented, and Cliff and I and the other men studied poetry, something much less ephemeral than permission to leave. Inevitably I think about the others: Ray—still inside and getting Alzheimer's. I saw him this week—he remembered me but I can do little more than welcome him to the class. A few months ago Ella called. After sixteen years outside, Stan had taken his life, so ruthless was the pain. I shared it with the men in the workshop but it was like sharing a ghost of the man I knew.

Debby and I went to see Art. He is in a rehabilitation facility: the shaking that precipitated his slow withdrawal from work has bloomed into Parkinson's and now his body is failing. His mind, however, has not fallen from anything. He has lightning awareness and his eyes tell us of his penetrating knowledge. He holds us close and shares, "I have been on a journey and it is not over." His voice is soft from the loss of muscle tone. He holds us like we are family with whom there is nothing to say, nothing but touch to assuage this day. Later, I call his partner, Darrin, a man who by now has learned the most sacred lesson from Art: friendship will build anything. He tells me Art has given his name to the business, given his credibility to Darrin's future. Even in this wheelchair, Art is giving to others.

Many chapters have closed in the years since I started to record this journey through a burnished land. A land that, for many, could as easily be Niger, or the Transvaal, or the Mojave, this desert of no recent desire. Several years ago when they were trying to put the nation's nuclear waste in Yucca Mountain, I wrote a poem with this line: "Nevada is never on the map, not now, / not ever." Writers have tried to give this place a name, but it is the absence of a name we recognize.

I often think it would be different if the desert's beauty was readily understood. People would not disguise it in transit or conversation about playas of alkaline dust. People would come here with a purpose, like our ancestors, like the Clovis Culture, like someone who needed this place. The paradox is most of us who live here like this place. We do not long to be elsewhere. Elsewhere is anywhere but here, so the desert can be almost anything to those who do not call this land home. We, its residents, can be anonymous like rain or sand, and then we resume our daily lives, try to create the story of this place and our lives in it.

I don't believe the story can be told; it must be inferred. Maybe there has been a thread I laid down to follow. Maybe it extends to the mountains above Lone Pine where Jess and I first hiked together. Maybe it is snaking its way south to my family in Southern California, maybe one of us will follow the discreet path of this thread and it will lead to the story that we become.

I began in the warmth of saffron light. I close this day in its warmth four years on. Light that cannot be described and light that comforts still.

Anthem for a Burnished Land

If we cannot unravel the drift of days
to mark the aspen with what strength remains—

not an idea of this dry, dry place
but what we do for work, whether field

or factory, what we imagine
this labor in sand and rock to mean:

and although the precise demeanor of doubt
is never far in this incalculable mountain and desert—

it is here we make our home, here we choose
the marbled canyon of our ancestors.

This day, unlike any other,
is the moment of redress: our burnished land

has suffered, but not without lament—
and its people, you and I, feather or cone,

reach for the trusted and damned alike,
to affirm what has been given.

It has always been up to us:
a generation for whom dust and wind

define the seeds of family—
whether child or mother, stone or river,

we begin this praise and praise again,
that what is done, be done for those to come.

STG

Index

Abbey, Edward *(Desert Solitaire)*, 98
Al-Azzawi, Fadhil, 229-30
American Flats: squatters in, 157-60; homeowners in, 158-59; as metaphor for quiet and calm, 163
Anaconda mine: impact of closing of, 12-13
Anaho Island, 180; as bird sanctuary, 20
Angora Fire, 225
Army Pass, 35
art, 41, 58, 194; challenges of, 53-54; need for, 55, 58, 91; place of, in community, 56; process of, 90, 91; value of, in Nevada, 154-55; Samuel Beckett on, 89
artists: and the Comstock, 209; vision of, 58
Austin, 193

Barnhart, Barbara, 17
baseball: in Virginia City, 121-20; and weather, 25; coaches, 128; in rural Nevada, 127, 128-29; high school, 124-27, 128; value of, to rural Nevada children, 127-28
basketball: in rural Nevada, 128-29
Bebbe, Lucius, 10
Black Rock Press, 207
Blesse, Robert, 207
Board of Pardons, Nevada; pardon hearing at, 85-89
books: and electronic media, 234-35; value of, 233-35
Bouldin, Lucy, 232
Boyd, Cindy, 73-74, 77
Brewer, Ken *(Whale Song; A Poet's Journey into Cancer)*, 62, 63-64
brothels, legal: in Nevada, 169
Bucket of Blood, 219
Bush, Barbara, 136

California State University, Fullerton: author at, 37
California: Nevada in the shadow of, 179-80

Camp Richardson, 82

Celtic Festival, 145

change: achieving, 49, 53-54, 57; consequences of, 152; fear of, 47

charity model: effects of, 49

child care: need for, in Virginia City, 45; center, 45

children: raising of, 146

City of Joy (movie), 243

Classroom on Wheels, 73-74, 197

Clemens, Samuel (Mark Twain), 10, 11, 154, 211, 212

Clerico, Bob, 136

Clovis Culture, 194, 251

Cobb Mansion, 219

Coleville, 128

commerce, local: key to success of, 219

community: building of, 56, 57, 197, 213; and response to crisis, 226; how work gets done in, 250

Community Chest (Virginia City): 49, 53, 125, 131, 137, 220-21, 249, 250; and community center, 152, 154; challenges of, 175, 176; decision to start, 43-44; expansion of, 50-51, 56, 73-74; finances of, 44, 72, 57, 58-59, 72-73, 149-52; and Global Voice project, 132-33, 135; guiding principles of, 75-76, 77; and legislative process, 54-55, 58-59; and library, 231-32; mission of, 232; as mentors, 74-75; need for, 45-46; repairs to building, 71-72; threats to, 77. *See also* Virginia City community center

Comstock Arts Council, 218-19

Comstock Cemetery Foundation, 217

Comstock: landscape of, 9, 10, 11, 12, 179, 214; challenges of living in, 10, 13, 27; light in, 10, 11; open mine shafts in, 116, 117; outsiders' perceptions of, 211; spring in, 237

Conforte, Joe, 170

counseling: practice of, 167

Covington, Mary Works, 220

Cowee, Bill, 206

Creel Station, 21

Crystal Bar, 217

Cummings, Nancy, 232, 234

DeQuille, Dan, 10
Desert Wood: An Anthology of Nevada Poets, 31
desert: beauty of, 251; living in, 13, 179-84
Devil's Gate, 210, 245
Dini, Joe, 55
Doten, Alf, 10
Dunn, Diane, 58

education: and at-risk children, 17; and homeless children, 49
Escobedo, Jacob, 58
exchange students: in Virginia City, 132-33, 140-41

faith: importance of, in sustaining effort, 54, 176
Fallon, 14
family values: teaching of, 136
fire: danger of, on the Comstock, 223-28, 229, 230
Firemen's Museum, 217
Fischer, Rich, 81
fishing, 40. *See also* Hayashi, Jess: fishing with
Fourth Ward School Museum, 217
free dental clinic, 237-39, 240-41
Frost, Robert, 128

Genasci, John, 17
Gilbertson, Tom, 56, 58, 206
Gold Hill, 210, 211, 245
Great Basin: landscape of, 179-84, 193-96; living in, 193, 194, 195
Greiner's Bend, 245
Griffin, Cody, 33, 99, 125-26, 134-36, 162, 204, 211; birth of, 30;
    as poster image, 50; and music study, 118-19; and baseball, 126-
    27
Griffin, Debby Loesch, 11, 23-24, 28-29, 30, 38, 39, 41, 43, 44, 45,
    47, 48, 99, 131, 132, 133-34, 135, 137, 142, 170, 175, 176-77,
    210-11, 224, 231, 246, 247; education and early career of, 16,
    17, 148; work of, in schools, 135
Griffin, Nevada, 18, 30, 33, 117, 158, 162, 250-51; birth of, 28-29;
    naming of, 29; and Jess Hayashi, 81, 93-94; and baseball, 124-26;

and school, 134-35; and sinkhole, 114, 115, 116
Griffin, Shaun: as poet, 13; writing of, 30-31; education of, 37

Hannifan, Art, 44, 56, 150, 197, 198, 201-202, 224, 251
Hayashi, Jess, 22, 29-30, 31, 33-35, 39-41, 79-81, 183, 252; and
    school for at-risk children, 14-15, 37-40, 80; fishing with, 19-
    20, 33-34, 41, 82; hiking with, 35-36; and cancer, 93-100; impact
    of death of, 175-76, 177
Heaney, Seamus, 90
high desert: beauty of, 214; transience of, 154
Highway 50, 11, 183, 193-94, 237
Hixson, Lisa, 17, 25, 176-77; death of, 133-34
Hobart Lake Reservoir, 33-36, 80, 81, 161
Homeless Youth Education program, 44, 48, 49, 74
homelessness: in Nevada, 159, 160-61; attitudes toward, 46-47, 49;
    and children, 46
horses, wild, 13, 161, 237
Houston Minerals Pit, 210
hunger: and poverty, 50
Hungry Miner, 218

identity: and the West, 12

J & T Basque Restaurant, 125
Jarbidge: annual barbeque in, 227
jazz: in Virginia City, 219-20
Jean LeGassick, 209
Joe (logger): 38-39, 41, 99; and cancer, 81, 82-84
Jumbo Grade, 33, 161-62

Kittredge, William (*The Last Best Place*), 212
Kizer, Carolyn, 203
Koch, Kenneth, 43
Koch, Merle and Michele, 219, 220
Kreyeski, Karen, 55, 136, 209

Lahontan cutthroat trout, 20

Lake Lahontan, 14
Lake Tahoe, 27
lakes, landlocked: in Great Basin, 21
Lane, Gordon, 169, 218
LaVake, Squeek, 118-19, 232, 234
Laxalt, Monique, 34
Laxalt, Robert, 34, 155
Leong, Lynn, 169, 218
Lewiston Dam: salmon spawning at, 39-40
library: closure of, in Virginia City, 231-32; children's, 232; and
    community, 232; value of, 233, 234-35
light: in the Comstock, 9, 11; in Yerington valley, 13
Little League: in Virginia City, 121-25; social role of, in small
    towns, 125
Loesch, Bob, 142-43, 144, 146, 228
Loesch, Gladys, 29, 142, 228-29
Longchamps, Joanne de, 195
Lyon County, 169, 211

Magistrali, Marta, 58
magpie funeral, 168
Mandelstam, Nadezhda (*Hope Against Hope*), 88
Manzanar (internment camp), 79-80
Mark Twain. *See* Clemens, Samuel
Marks, Bill and Margaret, 217
Marlette Lake, 34, 161
McGill, Christy, 154, 238, 239, 240
medical care: need for, in rural areas, 238-40, 243
Medical Outreach Response Event (MORE), 237-41
Meschery, Tom, 206
Midas, 181
Milosz, Czeslaw: on poetry, 69
Mina, 180, 195
mineshafts: on the Comstock, 116, 117
mining: and community in the West, 212; history of, on the
    Comstock, 211, 246; impact of, in the West, 211-12; new
    open-pit mine near Virginia City, 210-14

Montana, Shannon, 74, 77
Mount Davidson, 12, 24
Muir, Edwin, 89
Mulligan, John, 77

Neruda, Pablo, 65, 168-69
Nevada Board of Pardons, 85-89
Nevada State Prison (Carson City), 66
Nevada: boom and bust communities in, 213; landscape of, 12, 14; realities of life in, 154
Nichols, John *(The Milagro Beanfield War)*, 151
Nicholson, Jeff, 53, 54, 200, 209
non-profit work: in small towns, 46; challenges of, 54

open-pit mining: resumption of, on the Comstock, 209-10; and speculation, 211-13

Pahmeier, Gailmarie, 206
Paiute Indians: reservation of, 20; fishing as historic livelihood of, 21
Parlocha, Bob, 29
Patchen, Kenneth, 221
Pecoraro, Denis, 218
Perkins, Frances: on poverty, 50
Piper's Opera House, 217
poetry: act of, 85; Adrienne Rich on, 89; and staying alive, 91; need to write, 54; sustaining power of, 233; teaching of, 240; uses of, 90. *See also* prison poetry program
politics, local: in small towns, 46; working with, 48; and poverty, 49, 50
poverty: attitudes toward, in Virginia City, 47-48; and systems that maintain it, 49; fear of, 46, 48
Prater, Chris, 136
Preece, Nolan, 206-207
press, freedom of, 47
prison poetry program, 56, 87, 88, 89, 206, 233; description of, 61-69; effects of, 90-92; teaching at, 250-51. *See also* prison poets

prison poets: Cliff, 64-65, 250-51; Darnell, 62-64, 66, 67-68, 87, 91; Johnny, 66-67, 68, 89, 91, 205-207; Preston, 68, 91; Ray, 67, 85-89, 91, 251; Stan, 203-205, 206, 251; Tillman, 68-69
Pursel, Loren and Sue, 220
Pyramid Lake, 19, 180; fishing in, 20-22; Paiute reservation at, 129; salinity of, 21, 22; wind at, 26-27

Razor Wire (prison literary journal), 56, 90-91, 205, 206
Red Dog Saloon, 220
Reid, Robert, 194
Reid, Senator Harry, 44, 149, 150, 152, 153, 198
Remote Area Medical (RAM), 240
Rich, Adrienne: on writing poetry, 89
Roasting House, 219
Roughing It, 10, 211, 212. *See also* Clemens, Samuel

San Francisco: homelessness in, 47
Schoen, Erik, 76, 77, 152, 154, 239
school board: in Virginia City, 47
Schrank, Ric, 135-36, 209
Scott, Paula, 74, 76, 77
Sepúlveda, Emma, 77
Sharon House, 169, 218
shoe tree, 181
Short, Gary, 27-28, 58, 157, 158, 159-60, 206
Silver Stope, 219, 220
sinkholes: in Virginia City, 114-16
Six Mile Canyon, 183
small towns: attitude of, toward homeless children, 46; limitations of living in, for children, 131, 135
Smith, Annick, 212
Smith Creek Valley, 181, 182
Smith Valley, 125
Snake Valley, 194
Snowmelt, 31, 55
social change, 49, 57; rewards and challenges of, 43-44; process of, 53, 54

South Africa: schools in, 136

squatters: on the Comstock, 157-60. *See also* homelessness

St. Mary's Art Center, 217

Stanford University: Griffins at, 28-30, 48

Steinbeck, John *(The Log from the Sea of Cortez)*, 98

Stone Mother: story of, 26-27

Storey, Captain: massacre of, by Paiutes, 20

Storey County, 153, 211; justice in, 169-71; population of, 45-46; poverty in, 45-46, 47; need for human services in, 44-45, 50; legal prostitution in, 169-70

Strand, Mark, 214

success: search for, 36-37

Sun Mountain Artworks Gallery, 56, 66, 206, 218

tarantulas: migration of, 245-46

Thomas, Dylan ("A Child's Christmas in Wales"), 61

Tonapah, 194-95

tourism: and economy of Virginia City, 215-17, 218, 220; impact of, 216-18; musical, in Virginia City, 220

tourists: interaction with, 215-18

Truckee River, 21, 22

Turman, Tom, 205, 206

Uncle Pat, 218

Union Brewery, 165, 166, 169, 218, 219

University of Nevada, Reno: Debby Griffin at, 30

Varga, Billy, 111-15, 116

Vietnam: Reflexes and Reflections, 56

Virginia City: decision to live in, 10, 23; history of, 10, 11; historic preservation in, 217; businesses in, 218-19; changes to, from open-pit mine, 213; and Mark Twain, 10; closure of library in, 231-35; education in, 117-18, 135-36; poverty in, 45; racial intolerance in, 141; sinkhole in, 114; skate park in, 151; and tourists, 215-16; unemployment in, 111

Virginia City community center, 200-202, 246, 249-51; design of, 54, 56; funding of, 55, 56, 149-54, 198-99, 200-201; need for, 44,

197-98; and politics, 58, 153; and free clinic, 237-41; and
library, 234; children's library in, 232
Virginia City: local characters, 111-14; Butch, 171-74; Donovan,
165-68; Jake, 139-42, 144, 145-46, 147; Louie, 168-69, 170, 171;
Sheila, 173
volunteering: value of, for children, 131
Volunteers in Service to America (VISTA), 44, 74

Walden's Coffee House, 218
Walker Lake, 180
Washoe Club, 169
Washoe Valley, 16, 17
water: in Nevada, 14; sources of, for Comstock, 34, 161; and Truckee
River, 21
Wesner, Ben and Karen, 58, 98, 99, 210, 248
Wesner, Ben, 225
Wesner, Karen, 10, 81
West: meaning of, 155
Western Nevada College, 10, 12, 61
Williamson, Larry, 57-58
wind: on the Comstock, 23-26, 27, 31; causes of, 24, 28; Santa Anas,
24; termination winds (Washington State), 24
Winnemucca, Sarah, 200
winter: on the Comstock, 9-10
Woodsmoke, Wind, and the Peregrine, 68
Wordsworth, William, 89, 90

Yerington, 12, 125; living and teaching in, 14-16, 37; landscape of,
13
Yucca Mountain, 251

Also by Shaun T. Griffin

Poetry

This Is What the Desert Surrenders: New and Selected Poems
Woodsmoke, Wind, and the Peregrine
Winter in Pediatrics
Bathing in the River of Ashes
Snowmelt

Limited Editions

Driving the Tender Desert Home
Under Red-Tailed Sky
Words I Lost at Birth

Editions

From Sorrow's Well: The Poetry of Hayden Carruth
The River Underground: An Anthology of Nevada Fiction
Torn by Light: Selected Poems of Joanne de Longchamps
Desert Wood: An Anthology of Nevada Poets

Translation

Death to Silence (Muerte al silencio). Poems by Emma Sepúlveda